COLLECTOR'S GUIDE TO
ART DECO
SECOND EDITION
IDENTIFICATION & VALUES

MARY FRANK GASTON

COLLECTOR BOOKS
A Division of Schroeder Publishing Co., Inc.

The current values in this book should be used only as a guide. They are not intended to set prices, which vary from one section of the country to another. Auction prices as well as dealer prices vary greatly and are affected by condition as well as demand. Neither the author nor the publisher assumes responsibility for any losses that might be incurred as a result of consulting this guide.

Searching For A Publisher?

We are always looking for knowledgeable people considered to be experts within their fields. If you feel that there is a real need for a book on your collectible subject and have a large comprehensive collection, contact Collector Books.

On the Cover: Top left: Redwing Ceramic Pitchers & Tray, $175.00–225.00 set. Top right: Hutschenreuther porcelain Tigers, $700.00–800.00. Middle left: French bronze and silver Vase, $600.00–700.00. Middle right: 1939 World's Fair Saturn Lamp, $325.00–375.00. Bottom: Ceramic Clock, $175.00–225.00.

Cover design by Beth Summers
Book design by Mary Ann Dorris

COLLECTOR BOOKS
P.O. Box 3009
Paducah, Kentucky 42002-3009

Copyright © 1997 by Mary Frank Gaston
Values updated, 2000

Contents

Other Books by Mary Frank Gaston

Collector's Encyclopedia of Limoges Porcelain...$24.95

Collector's Encyclopedia of R. S. Prussia, First Series...$24.95

Collector's Encyclopedia of R. S. Prussia, Second Series..$24.95

Collector's Encyclopedia of R. S. Prussia, Third Series...$24.95

Collector's Encyclopedia of R. S. Prussia, Fourth Series...$24.95

Blue Willow, Revised Second Edition...$14.95

Collector's Encyclopedia of Flow Blue China, First Series..$19.95

Collector's Encyclopedia of Flow Blue China, Second Series...$24.95

Antique Brass & Copper..$16.95

Collector's Encyclopedia of Knowles, Taylor & Knowles China...$24.95

The titles may be ordered from the author or the publisher. Include $2.00 each for postage and handling.

Mary Frank Gaston
P.O. Box 342
Bryan, TX 77806

Collector Books
P.O. Box 3009
Paducah, KY 42002 – 3009

In Memory of Vera

who lived the era

1908 – 1997

Acknowledgments

There are a number of people I would like to thank for their help and cooperation on this edition. First, I thank Chris Clark and Urban Cummings, Palo Alto, California, who wrote to me after the first edition was published. They were instrumental in my considering more extended work on Art Deco. Jerry and I enjoyed our visits with Chris and Urban, talking "Deco" and gaining from their expertise in the field, especially concerning the Ronson Company. Urban's book on that topic was published in 1994. It is a needed and very useful reference for not only Ronson collectors, but also for others interested in tobacciana in particular and to Deco collectors in general. I am very pleased to have been able to photograph and include pieces in this edition from Chris and Urban's collection. Their contributions were not limited to lighters, but included an assortment of pieces such as dress accessories, figures, and incense burners as well.

Second, I thank Barbara and Pete Nicholson and their daughter, Cerise Gideon. Barbara and Pete were contributors to the first book and are avid Deco collectors. We photographed pieces at their shop which was in Austin, Texas, at that time. Now, their shop, Decades, is located in Georgetown, Texas. Cerise shares their interest and has joined them in the business. A number of items, including many of the compacts, featured here are from the Nicholson–Gideon collection.

Third, I thank Bobby G. Green, Past Revisited Antiques, who also was a contributor to the first book. Bobby exhibits at antique shows in Texas and is often in Bryan. He always kindly lets me dismantle his booth to photograph examples. He also is helpful in introducing me to other dealers who have interesting pieces at the shows. A large number of the American art pottery pieces which are illustrated here are from Bobby's collection.

I also thank Greg Vitale, Antiques Unlimited, Palo Alto, California, for providing access to his wide array of Deco items. Greg pointed out special pieces and offered pertinent information about them. Some of the chrome items shown are from his collection. Chrome is difficult to photograph, and one piece gives a pretty good view of Greg's shop and the photographer! The piece was so neat that I decided to include it — Jerry and all — see if you can find it!

Thanks also to Tony Craig, ASC DECO, Dallas, Texas. Tony offers a nice selection of Deco items, ranging from clocks and figures to jewelry and china.

He provided a great space for photographing in his back room, and was very helpful in advising on specific pieces which would be of interest to collectors. I am pleased to include a number of examples from his shop.

Additional thanks to the following contributors who either permitted me to photograph pieces from their exhibits at antique shows or who corresponded with me and sent photographs which have been included:

Anthony Agard
John Allen, Dallas, Texas
Michael Anderson
Diane Beck
Edda Biesterfeld
Ron Capers
Chris Crain
Dorothy Coates
Juanita and Alan Conover, J & A Collectibles, Penrose, Colorado
Shirley and Jerry Daugherty, Daugherty's Antiques, Lincoln, Nebraska
Wallace J. Ehrlich
Judy Ellis
Marcy and Bob Grabko, Rochester, Minnesota
Margaret Harlan
Robert A. Hase
Chyril Hoke
Bill Holloway
Linda and Marion Katz, Golden Eye Gallery, Katy, Texas
Jennifer McClaflin
Ward McCoy
Linda Richard, College Station, Texas
Eilis McLoughlin
Roberta Patterson
Lynn Ann Payne, Fort Worth, Texas
Frances Simmert
Pam Trammel
Carole Watkins
Nancy and Denver Wetzel
Sylvia and Joe Wilson, Winters, Texas
Joyce Witmer
Anita and Clarence Woods, Gramma's Attic, Tulsa, Oklahoma
Kathleen Yard
Joseph R. Young

I thank my husband, Jerry, who photographed most of the pieces for this edition. I also thank him for keeping his day job so that I can write about my collecting interests!

I thank my publisher, Billy Schroeder, Jr., Collector Books, for publishing this revised edition.

I thank Lisa C. Stroup, my editor, and her fine staff, for all the varied tasks they do to ensure an attractive finished product. I enjoy working with them very much.

Finally, I once again thank all of the contributors to the first edition of this book:

Barbara and Pete Nicholson (formerly Art Deco Adventure, Austin, Texas)

Jake Iseman and Dane Hawkins, Juxtaposition, Houston, Texas

The Thomas M. Crocker Collection

Dee's Uniques, Etc., Jefferson, Texas

Bobby G. Green, The Past Revisited, Abilene, Texas, and The Antique Center, San Antonio, Texas

The Antique Connection, San Antonio, Texas

Dorothy Ball, El Paso, Texas

C & M Enterprises, Houston, Texas

The Depot, New Braunfels, Texas

The Doubletree, Wimberly, Texas

George H. Dreyfus, L'Opera Antiques, Austin, Texas, and Beauvais, France

David Harris, Big D Bazaar, Dallas, Texas

Dianne Heath, Salmagundi, Amarillo, Texas

David F. Lebetter, Yesterdaze Mall, Abilene, Texas

House of Lowell, Houston, Texas

B. Lightsey, San Antonio, Texas

Mrs. J. G. McElvain, Dallas, Texas

The Main Place, San Antonio, Texas

Rosie O'Reilly, Austin, Texas

Fay Schoenfeld, San Antonio, Texas

The Uncommon Market, Dallas, Texas and

The Victory Antiques, Dallas, Texas.

Preface

As a child of the 1940s, I grew up during the waning years of what is now called the Art Deco period. Various and sundry remnants from that past which happened to linger on the scene in the way of household objects, clothing, and jewelry evidently made a lasting impression on me. I always seem to have had a nostalgic interest in them. Although perhaps I was aware of "Deco" before "collecting Deco was cool," unfortunately I did not get in on the ground floor, so to speak, and capture prime examples by famous artists and designers of the era. This was because I lacked both the knowledge and the resources!

In fact, once Art Deco hit the collectibles scene during the late 1960s and early 1970s, it became rather abruptly apparent that my Deco, according to some, was not considered real Deco. My "rhythm" dancing girl pot metal lamp, red cocktail glasses with chrome stems, and especially my black glass nude ashtray would fall under the heading of "kitsch," according to some writers on the subject.

Nonetheless my interest in such items did not diminish. Over the last several years, as I have traveled around the country gathering information for other books on other topics, I have seen a dramatic increase in similar types of articles appearing on the market. This "secondary" level of Art Deco can be found at antique malls and shows. By and large, examples from this market are part of the large supply of mass-produced and mass-marketed items made during the 1920s and 1930s. Such pieces imitated or resembled "modern" looks set forth in Europe during the second quarter of the twentieth century. Many were made in the United States by various china, glass, and metal companies. Deco stereotypes of angular shapes, geometric patterns, nude figures, and bold colors characterize most pieces. These qualities, rather than a particular company name or manufacturer, are sought by the average collector.

An abundant supply of a large variety of articles is available. Prices have increased over the last several years as more and more collectors join the ranks of Deco enthusiasts. Prices remain moderate, however, compared to prices obtained at the great auction houses for work by major designers and craftsmen of the period.

This book is not meant to be a literary reconstruction or detailed history of the period and its major contributors. That type of study has been very well done by others, especially Victor Arwas's *Art Deco*, Bevis Hillier's *Art Deco*, and Katherine Morrison McClinton's *Art Deco: A Guide for Collectors*. These books, as well as several other entries listed in the Bibliography, should be read by all Deco collectors.

This survey centers on the type of Deco currently found for sale at general antique and collectibles outlets. While most are representative of mass productions, some pieces by noted "names" of the period are sometimes found in such locations. I have included examples by French designers and manufacturers such as Sandoz, Daum, and Le Gras because they were available for sale and thus do comprise part of the average market place.

Since the first edition of this book was published in 1989, interest in Art Deco has continued to widen its grasp on collectors. Several shows and exhibits in various parts of the country are held each year which are devoted entirely to Art Deco, Art Moderne, or collectibles from the 20s, 30s, and 40s. A very large variety of striking, beautiful, and even amusing items are available.

While interest has spread, prices have also increased, but that is true for not just Deco items, but also for other antiques and consumer goods. Finding a bargain is not easy, but the search for one keeps us hopeful!

In this revised edition, the ten categories of Art Deco collectibles have been expanded illustrating more examples in each. Each section is prefaced with brief introductory remarks about the category. The value ranges have been included in the captions of the photographs. A notation of (mc) indicates the value is for the piece in mint condition. The Manufacturer Index helps locate examples of a particular company.

At the end of this edition, a few reproductions of bronze figures are illustrated. Such items are often found on the antique market. While advanced collectors are knowledgeable of their existence, new collectors should be aware as well.

I hope you, too, continue to enjoy Deco for the fun of it!

Mary Frank Gaston
P.O. Box 342
Bryan, TX 77806

For all correspondence, please include a self-addressed, stamped envelope.

Origins and Development of Art Deco

L' Exposition International des Arts Décoratifs et Industriels Modernes was held in Paris, France, from April to October in 1925. This international exhibit was arranged for the purpose of showing the work of current artists, craftsmen, and designers who attempted to project a view of contemporary and future trends in artistic decoration. The event had been planned much earlier, but the onset and aftermath of World War I caused the Exposition to be postponed until 1925. As the title implied, the purpose of the Exposition was to demonstrate that elements of art and industrial techniques could be combined as applied art to make both utilitarian and attractive products. These were desirable to accommodate the changing life styles occurring because of the industrial progress of the twentieth century.

Countries which participated at the Exposition set up pavilions to house the respective displays of their selected artisans. France, along with Austria, Belgium, Czechoslovakia, Denmark, England, Greece, Holland, Italy, Japan, Monaco, Poland, Russia, Spain, Sweden, and Turkey were represented. Two major countries did not participate. Germany was not invited because of the strained relations resulting from the war. The United States did not accept the invitation because according to "Herbert Hoover...there was no modern art in the United States" (Arwas, p14). For a full description of the 1925 Exposition, see the book by Frank Scarlett and Marjorie Townley (*Arts Décoratifs 1925*, London: St. Martins Press, 1975).

The 1925 Exposition captured the current world of design and had a profound influence on design over the succeeding years. The styles and designs of the work shown at the Exposition were not identical. As years passed, the styles displayed in 1925 were emulated, but they were not copied slavishly or duplicated precisely. In fact, varied interpretations and other innovative designs emerged during the following years. The style highlighted in 1925 served as the basis for developing the "modern" look of the decorative arts over the next generation.

Because of assorted opinions about Art Deco, its history is controversial. Numerous individuals and groups, various schools of design, many social and world events, and several philosophical ideas or "isms" are considered instrumental in the development of Art Deco. A wealth of material has been written on these various aspects of the suject.

It is not my purpose to present a detailed historical survey. Rather, readers are encouraged to consult the selected entries in the Bibliography for a thorough review of Art Deco's complex background.

Rarely does a consensus exist about the precise dates of artistic or historical periods. Prior developments are important and will inevitably lead to some point that later is identified as the beginning of the period. The literature which describes the development of the Art Deco style has several different views about when the era began and ended and about where and why it originated. There is even disagreement about what Art Deco actually is.

Art Deco is sometimes seen as a reaction against Art Nouveau, the immediately preceding period of decorative design (1890s – 1914). Art Nouveau is a style based on romantic and naturalistic images, dominated by a graceful, curvilinear line. It is highly decorative, having a sensuous, dreamy, more subtle quality than the gaudy ornamentation typically associated with the Victorian period.

Art Deco, in contrast, is often considered as an interpretation of the future based on the use of straight angles and clean lines without superfluous decoration. This opinion is contradicted by observers who point out that early Art Deco did not fit that description. It was neither all lines and angles nor were all examples plain and austere. These writers believe Art Deco grew out of Art Nouveau or was a refinement of that earlier style. They emphasize that early pieces often were richly executed with lavish materials and were quite luxurious.

Some authors describe Art Deco as being a "new art" which did not imitate previous designs. Critics of that view believe that the "true" Art Deco was derived from the restrained neo-classical eighteenth century styles. Another view is that Art Deco borrowed from cultures such as the Egyptian, African, and American Indian.

In addition to the origin and characteristics of style, the original audience for Art Deco is debatable. On the one hand, it is seen as intended for the wealthy. Some experts accept only the work of the top designers and craftsmen as being representative of true Art Deco. Certain individuals who exhibited at the Paris Exposition are usually cited as the most important names associated with the style. Others insist the style was developed primarily for the middle classes. Mass-produced wares which strived to imitate the modern trends of the 1920s and 1930s are scorned by some. Such examples are often lumped under the heading of "kitsch," a German term literally defined as "trash," or the debasement of original works. Today, however, many of those items have become extremely collectible and comprise the major part of many collections.

Another dispute in the literature is that Art Deco

is synonymous with France. Deco items of French origin are considered superior to examples from other countries. France, in fact, is usually considered the birthplace of Art Deco, especially because of the 1925 Exposition. Yet knowledgeable writers trace its development through other European centers such as Austria and Germany. Indeed, the list of countries exhibiting at the 1925 Exposition is evidence that craftsmen in many countries were designing their work simultaneously along lines which now are identified as Art Deco. Thus, it is apparent that other countries expressed their own views of modern design. And while the United States did not participate in the 1925 event, that certainly does not mean that modern design was not developing here as well.

Purists say Art Deco ended in 1925, with the peak of the style culminating in the Paris Exposition. They do not believe that the work which followed was worthy of the name. Others, less dogmatic, differentiate between "Art Deco" and "Art Moderne." Art Deco would include design up to 1925, and Art Moderne would describe the style that followed after that year and on into the 1930s. This clear division separates the components of elegant style following Art Nouveau from the purely angular and stark designs brought forth in the late 1920s.

Other critics maintain that Art Deco includes the entire period of the 1920s through the 1940s. Alternatively, Art Deco is referred to as the style popular between two World Wars — 1918 –1940. Other definitions of the era confine the period between the years of 1925, the date of the initial French exhibit, and 1940.

If the general consensus is that 1940 or World War II signifies the end of the main production of Art Deco, then World War I is usually considered the most important event influencing the development of the Art Deco period. Life styles certainly changed during and after the war. Servants left their positions to fight, or in the case of women, work for the war effort. The sons and daughters of the wealthy also became involved in wartime activities. After the war, many former domestics refused to return "downstairs," seeking more regular jobs and their own living quarters. Because of the war, both servant class and upper class women began to become more independent. A desire to enjoy life and a relaxation of morals are also often cited as important consequences of the war. A middle class began to emerge which demanded a release from the encumbered Victorian way of life steeped in heavy traditions, pious attitudes, and elaborate rituals of dressing, entertaining, and running households.

Although World War I might be the focal point for

recognizing a change in the world's life styles, other important factors also occurred before and after the war which helped bring about this change. The first 40 years of the twentieth century witnessed unsurpassed progress in industry which led to a more convenient way of life in all areas: from horse and buggy to automobile, train, and plane, from gas lighting to electricity; from outdoor to indoor plumbing; from hand delivered calling cards to telephone, telegram, and radio. This period of rapid change in transportation, communication, and manufacturing resulted in a smaller world, as is often quoted, by making distant people and places more accessible. But it also made the world larger for the average person by making more goods and services available and thereby allowing more individual freedom. It is not surprising that as life became more efficient, especially for the average person, all aspects of style and design were influenced.

In spite of the various views of its origin and development, Art Deco is a recognized age just as its immediate predecessors, the Victorian and Art Nouveau periods. Like those well known categories of collector interests, Art Deco, too, has become firmly established. In 1965, a revival of the 1925 Exposition, *Les Annees '25*, was held in Paris. World attention once again took a look at what had been hailed as modern in 1925. The success of this subsequent exhibit brought forth a new period for collectors. "Art Deco," derived from the lengthy French title of the original Exposition, quickly caught on as an apt descriptive term not only for the style showcased in 1925, but perhaps more importantly also evolved to identify the modernistic designs which were either continued or initiated after 1925 until the 1940s.

Today, auctions specialize in sales devoted to artifacts from the period. General price guides include Art Deco as a specific entry, listing a variety of examples and current prices fetched at auctions or in the collectibles market. As collector interest in the subject grew, the definition of Art Deco has expanded to include a much broader scope than purists might prefer.

Today, Art Deco is quite loosely interpreted to include a very wide range of objects from fine art to the mundane and produced as early as the first decade of the twentieth century until the beginning of the fifth decade. The style is characterized by several different elements of design which may include the following: an understated and restrained elegance; sharply angular and geometric lines, often void of any decoration; futuristic concepts; suggestions of speed and movement; both vivid and contrasting colors; Jazz age and Flapper influences; Aztec, African, and Egyptian cultural symbols; and certain materials which became popular such as

Bakelite, celluloid, chrome, and dark colored glass.

Anything which exhibits one or more of these traits is generally classified as part of the Art Deco period. It does not matter if it is an original work by a famous person or merely a mass-produced dime-store novelty. Consequently, and fortunately, Art Deco can be enjoyed by collectors as diverse as its many dimensions.

Serious wealthy collectors purchase creations by top designers, artists, and manufacturers identified with the early years of the era. Prices for such examples can easily mount to five figures. Many who like Deco cannot compete in that market. But as in other collecting areas, once the top of the line has been singled out and record prices paid for choice pieces, a second level of collecting surfaces which attracts a wider, though perhaps less affluent, group. Consequently, a middle ground of Deco collecting has arrived on the scene. From the offerings at shops and shows across the country, as well as a perusal of most general value surveys on the subject, interest in Art Deco with medium to moderate prices is quite strong.

While many pay thousands of dollars for Art Deco rarities and originals, perhaps seeing such purchases as investments and true works of art, there is also a growing number of enthusiasts who collect Art Deco for the fun of it! Possible future value is usually only a secondary consideration. Some might take issue with the assertion, but Art Deco is fun. Other collecting periods cannot really be characterized in that way. For instance, Victoriana is intriguing, and collectors search for the many necessities and unique items of everyday life, obsolete today, but vital at that time. Likewise, primitives are very interesting. Collectors seek the ingenuity of those individuals who had to fashion their own tools, dishes, and furniture from whatever materials were at hand. Such articles may be curiosities, but they would hardly be described as fun. Most items commonly associated with Art Deco today, however, usually evoke a smile or sense of amusement because of their exaggerated lines, bold colors, ultra sophisticated or irreverent nature, or cleverness of design.

The focus of this book is on a very general interpretation of Art Deco. It is intended for the collector who enjoys the vibrant spirit of Art Deco and who collects according to individual whimsy and moderate pocketbook, perhaps splurging at times on certain irresistible objects! Pieces illustrated include some examples by famous names with prices of over $1,000 but many other items are representative of the mass productions of numerous manufacturers. Those prices are certainly more now than when the articles were first produced, but they are still affordable. There are also other objects made by little known or unknown creators whose prices are quite nominal. Examples are not limited to items of French origin but include Deco from many other countries. Art Deco made in America, Czechoslovakia, and Japan is especially becoming more and more popular with collectors. Concentration on Deco shapes and motifs instead of particular designers or manufacturers can often yield unexpected Art Deco treasures!

In the photographs, decorative objects for the home and personal accessories are grouped under 10 categories which comprise some of the most popular Art Deco collectibles. These categories are not meant to be comprehensive. The broad scope of the subject does not make such a survey possible. Hopefully, a sample of items in these categories will serve to suggest other Deco collecting possibilities as well as Art Deco's open ended nature. The majority of examples were available on the open market: that is, items sold at antique shops and shows rather than from private collections or museums. A price range has been established for individual items based not only on what the dealer was asking for the piece but from information gathered from numerous other sources on similar or identical pieces.

From the items featured, certain earmarks of what is currently collected as Art Deco can be seen. For instance, typical subjects of decoration are dominated by human figures either in a nude or semi-nude state, and depictions of the sun, moon, and earth are prevalent. Suggestions of the future and of speed are shown either by items actually shaped in the form of an airplane, ship, or rocket, or as a decorative motif.

All types of geometric shapes and lines can be found incorporated into the designs of most objects. The cube, triangle, or pyramid, and stepped or zig-zagged lines are common. Crescent or half-moon shapes made into rainbows or fans, spheres representing the world, and many sundry other shapes such as a diamond, cylinder, ellipse or oval, square, hexagon, and octagon stand out as well.

Repetitive, tangential, overlapping, and ziggurat patterns plus juxtaposed designs appear in the design or decor of a number of pieces. Also quite noticeable are many different construction materials, ranging from ceramic, glass, ivory, marble, metals, and wood to metal alloys and synthetics. From the Art Deco pictured, perhaps it will also be clear why Art Deco often is described not only by such words as chic, clever, elegant, smart, sophisticated, streamlined, and tailored, but also as amusing, flippant, risqué, and fun!

Bar Ware

The "cocktail" derived from the French term for mixed alcoholic beverages, *coquetel*, was an integral part of the Deco era. The spirit of the fancy before-dinner mixed drink was well suited to the carefree and relaxed atmosphere of the 1920s, but its popularity endured during the troublesome years of the Depression and World War II. The custom offered escape perhaps at one point in the day from the worries at home and abroad. Today, the cocktail hour remains a fixed part of the social scene.

The Volstead Act (Prohibition) was passed by Americans in 1920, and the law was not repealed until 1933 — 13 long years. It is interesting to note that during that time, however, imbibing was anything but dormant! Home bars became a part of the modern life, from a modest card table to lavish built-in bars fitted with all the necessities for mixing and serving drinks. Of particular interest to collectors are the portable bars. These cabinets were quite compact and doubled as a piece of furniture. They were well suited to restricted living quarters. These bars were usually made of wood and designed either with open or hidden storage compartments for bottles and stemware. The portable bars usually had some space, either on top, recessed, or pull out, which could be used for mixing drinks.

While the most affluent hired bartenders or butlers, the middle class host tended his own bar or allowed the guests to serve themselves. The portable bars worked well for small apartments and houses, and they are really no less useful today. French and English import houses offer a variety of styles.

A rather large variety of accessories was required to maintain a well stocked and fitted bar to accommodate ones' guests! Ice buckets, cocktail shakers, soda dispensers, decanters, tumblers, stems, and swizzle sticks were just some of the basics. Such items also hold an interest for collectors. Because cocktails were actually a product of the era, the majority of bar ware items usually has some identifying characteristic associated with Deco style. In fact, to many collectors, bar ware is a particular facet of Deco.

While lending a special decor to one's entertainment center as well as a nostalgic bit of the past, bar ware accessories are often still quite usable. Many items were made either of heavy glass or chrome, both durable with non-rusting properties. Chrome was especially used for shakers, dispensers, and trays. The metal with its shiny mirrored surface adapted well to the modern look.

Chrome bar ware made by the Chase Company of Waterbury, Connecticut, seems to dominate the market. Examples are usually marked and prices for Chase pieces are related to the uniqueness of the object.

Wide mouthed cocktail tumblers or stems made in clear glass were fashionable during the early years, but colored glass became popular during the late 1920s and 1930s. Ruby red, cobalt blue, and emerald or jade green bar glasses are eagerly sought by collectors. American Depression era glass factories contributed assorted items to this category. Colored glass combined with chrome added a smart note to bar ware items, too.

The ingenuity and creativity of bar ware manufacturers is apparent in some of the examples shown in this section. The "global" liqueur set, the "Zepplin" bar, and the "dancing nude" cocktail stem definitely define several of the preoccupations of the era — world communication, speed, relaxed morals, and most of all, fun! Assembling an entertaining collection of Deco bar ware can be a very enjoyable hobby.

Plate 1. Manning Bowman Cocktail Shaker, 12"h, chrome with Bakelite lid, American. $150.00 – 175.00.

Plate 3. Century Cocktail Shaker, 12"h, chrome plated with red plastic finial on lid. $70.00 – 90.00.

Plate 2. Chase Cocktail Shaker, "Target" design, 12¼" h, polished chrome with white plastic lid. $80.00 – 100.00.

Plate 4. Chase Cocktail Set: "Gaiety" Shaker, 11½"h; 4 cups, 2"h, 4"d; tray, 15⅞"l, polished chrome with black bands decorating shaker. $150.00 – 175.00 set.

Plate 5. Farberware Krome-Kraft Cocktail Shaker, 11½"h, chrome with a hammered and plain design on body, black composition handle. $65.00 – 85.00. Cocktail stems, 6"h, amethyst glass inserts by Cambridge Glass Company, Cambridge, Ohio. $35.00 – 45.00 each.

Plate 6. Cocktail Shaker, chrome, 12"h, simple etched design of stylized grapes and leaves forms border on body, spout cover cork lined, unmarked. $60.00 – 75.00.

Plate 7. Kromaster Cocktail Shaker, 12"h, chrome, made with a pouring spout. $65.00 – 80.00.

Plate 8. Cocktail Shaker, 7½"h, dark green glass, molded spout, no lid. $60.00 – 70.00.

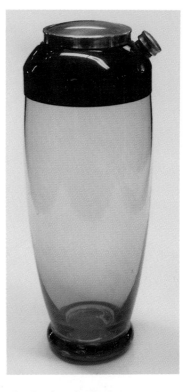

Plate 9. Cocktail Shaker, 10½"h, light green glass with black molded top, brass lid and spout cover. $90.00 – 110.00.

Plate 10. Fostoria Ice Bucket, 6"h x 5½"w, blue glass, metal handle, American. $80.00 – 100.00.

Plate 11. Ice Bucket, 6"h, glass, chrome handle, unmarked, American. $45.00 – 55.00.

Plate 12. Ice Bucket, 11"h, chrome, unmarked; cobalt blue glass insert, 8"d, by Hazel Atlas Glass Co., American. $90.00 – 100.00.

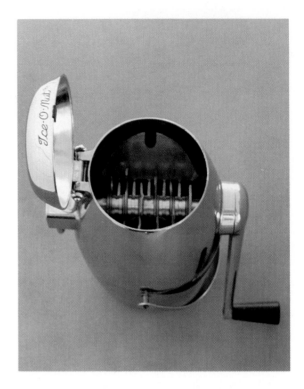

Plate 13. Ice Crusher/Bucket, 8½"h, chrome, marked "Bucketeer, Rival Mfg. Co." The "Ice-O-Mat" has a hand-turned crusher on top; the base twists off to form the bucket holder, American. $80.00 – 100.00.

Plate 14. Manning-Bowman Ice Tongs, 7½"l, chrome. $15.00 – 18.00.

Plate 15. Assorted Bar Items: right, Stirrer, 11"l, chrome and plastic; middle, Double Jigger, 2½"h, chrome; left, Jigger and Stirrer combination, 9"l, silverplate. $14.00 – 18.00 each.

Plate 16. Soda King Syphon Selzer Bottle, 12½", gold enameled body, American. $100.00 – 125.00.

Plate 17. Soda Dispenser, chrome, 9½"h, marked "Soda King, Made in U. S. A." $60.00 – 75.00.

Plate 18. Flask, 5½"l x 3h", radio design, chrome and black leather, tin lined, marked "Made in Germany." $25.00 – 35.00.

Plate 19. Cocktail Cup with cobalt blue glass insert, 2½"h, unmarked. $30.00 – 40.00. Chase "Blue Moon" Cocktail Cup, 3 ½"h. $25.00 – 35.00.

Plate 20. Shot Glass with bullet shaped case, 3"h, inscribed "Take a Shot," chrome, German. $35.00 – 45.00.

Plate 21. Tumblers, 3"h, sterling silver, flared mouth with large round base, marked "Cartier," American. $150.00 – 175.00 each.

Plate 22. Cocktail Stem fashioned with a mermaid in white glass supporting cobalt blue glass bowl with etched design; cobalt blue glass base; unmarked, American. $125.00 – 150.00.

Plate 23. Cambridge Glass Cocktail Stem, 6½"h, figural nude stem in forest green glass with clear glass bowl and base. $175.00 – 200.00.

Plate 24. Cocktail Stem, 5"h, dancing nude figure supports pink glass bowl, unmarked, American. $75.00 – 100.00.

Plate 25. Cocktail Stems, ruby red glass decorated with molded geometric designs, chrome stems, 3"h, marded "Stainless Chrome," American. $20.00 – 25.00 each.

Plate 26. Chrome Tray, 12½"l with black composition sides fitted with pink and green shot glasses, unmarked. $70.00 – 90.00 set.

Plate 27. Tray and Tumblers, dark green glass; tray accented with chrome handles and holders, American. $100.00 – 120.00 set.

Plate 28. Cocktail Shaker, 10"h; Czechoslovakian glass with silver deposit ring decor, chrome lid; matching tumblers in set of six. $220.00 – 240.00 set.

Plate 29. Decanter, 11"h; Glasses, 2¼"h, clear glass accented with red painted rings; unmarked, American. $50.00 – 65.00 set.

Plate 30. Liqueur Set, amber colored glass: Decanter, 10"h, four Tumblers, Czechoslovakian. $250.00 – 275.00 set.

Plate 31. Liqueur Set, chrome, 8½"h, 14"l overall. Two spheres (globes) function as Decanters, supported on pedestal bases and fitted with spigots. The attached handle forms holder for six Shot Glasses, four are light blue and two are clear, unmarked. $400.00 – 500.00 set.

Plate 32. Portable Bar, black and white Bakelite fitted with glass whiskey decanters and highball and shot glasses, unmarked. $300.00 – 400.00.

Plate 33. Liqueur Set encased in a replica of a bowling ball, 14"h overall; marbleized plastic with a finial of a bowler in gilded metal; chrome dispenser with red plastic lid; Shot Glasses trimmed with red, green, or blue applied glass rings; unmarked, American. $120.00 – 140.00 set.

Plate 34. Cocktail Set: Shaker, 11"h, Ice Bucket, 6¼"h; Shot Glasses and Tumblers, 3"h; clear and frosted glass with silver and chrome decor, unmarked. $125.00 – 150.00 set of 14 pieces.

Plate 35. Cocktail Glass decorated with antelopes on clear glass, unmarked. $15.00 – 20.00.

Plate 37. Parts of the Zepplin Bar: left to right, nested Tumblers, Cocktail Shaker, Ice Bucket; foreground, nested Stirrers and Lids for the Shaker, Ice Bucket and top cover. The container with the nested Stirrers attaches to the outer surface of the Zepplin (see preceding photograph).

Plate 36. The Zepplin Bar, chrome, 12"h, marked "Germany." The Zepplin airship was designed by the German Count, Ferdinand von Zepplin, who died in 1917. The Zepplin's futuristic shape inspired the creation of this Deco item. The following photograph shows how the Zepplin breaks down to furnish the essentials for concocting one's favorite cocktail! $2,500.00 – 3,000.00.

Plate 38. Cheese Board, 6½"d, wooden base, chrome cover with plastic handle, Chase. $75.00 – 100.00.

Plate 39. Cheese Dish: Tray, 14"d, domed cover, Chase. The original piece included a wooden cheese board. $100.00 – 125.00 (mc).

Plate 40. Tray, 16"l, 11½"w, cobalt blue glass and chrome, attributed to American designer, Norman Bel Geddes, manufactured by Revere Copper & Brass. $225.00 – 275.00.

Plate 41. Metal Tray, 12¾"d, painted silhouette of a nude dancer decorates center. $35.00 – 45.00.

Plate 42. Chase "Four-in Hand" Server, chrome with white plastic handle; middle trays swivel. $125.00 – 150.00.

Plate 43. Covered Server, 10"d, chrome with red Bakelite finial, German, $60.00 – 75.00.

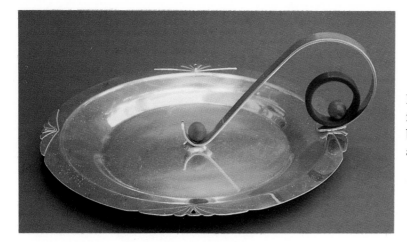

Plate 44. Chrome Serving Tray, round with incised design and cut-out work on outer border; scrolled handle with Bakelite accents, unmarked. $35.00 – 45.00.

Plate 45. Chrome Swan holds picks for olives and onions — basics for martinis, unmarked. $30.00 – 35.00.

Plate 46. "Pretzel Man" Server by Chase, 7½"h, 9"d; the figure is noted as a "high stepper" in the Chase catalog. He holds a tray aloft; originally 18"h incorporating a holder to carry pretzels or doughnuts (missing from this example); copper. $250.00 – 300.00 (mc).

Clocks

Mass productions in the clock industry during the early 1800s made some type of timepiece affordable for even the most modest household. Since Victorian times, clocks have been considered a necessity as well as a decorative object. Clocks are not only useful, they also are intriguing. Their intricate works and variety of encasements have contributed to their popularity throughout the ages. Initially clocks were expensive. By the 1920s, however, the average home had more than one clock to keep everyone on time! In addition to large grandfather clocks for the hall, mantel sets, and kitchen clocks, small table top varieties were made for the bedside, vanity, or writing desk.

Examples in this section show how some of the prominent Deco themes were used in clock design. It is apparent that clock manufacturers were aware of the prevailing trends in home furnishings. Angular shapes, concepts of flight and motion, and female or animal figures were part of the style or decoration of numerous clocks made to complement modern decor. These clocks were made from many different types of material, ranging from marble, bronze, brass, and silver to wood, glass, ceramic, celluloid, and plastic.

The French clocks were the most elaborate and those with figural adornments are especially sought by collectors. The figures were not always made of bronze although their finish may appear to be bronze. Metal alloys were used in the production of most available examples found today. These alloys are often referred to as pot metal, spelter, or white metal. In addition to bronze colors, other color finishes were used to coat the exteriors. Such examples, however, can rarely be purchased for less than several hundred dollars. French origin and extreme or "high" Deco design account for expensive prices.

Several of the mantel sets pictured have matching side panels. These were purely decorative and served no particular function except to flank each side of the clock. Side panels evidently have not survived all of the clocks which had them originally. While their absence does not detract from the clock itself, the panels often accentuate the overall Deco design.

Art Deco clocks can be one of the most costly categories for moderate spending collectors. Plain or less interesting specimens may still be $100 or more. Wooden shelf clocks with a simple rectangular or square shape are currently imported from abroad and may be purchased for less than $100. Beware that quite a few reproductions of Deco style clocks are also on the market. If you are interested in authentic examples from the period, check them out carefully. Most reproductions are inexpensive, have clean faces, no signs of wear on the case, and are in working condition (but many vintage ones are not!).

Plate 47. Clock, 15"l, 15"h, black marble and multicolored onyx, adorned with leaping gazelles made of white metal with brown and black finish; matching Side Panels, 7"l, 6½"h, cut with a steep stepped design, French. $1,400.00 – 1,600.00.

Plate 48. Clock with Side Panels, pink and white marble, semi-nude figure with stylized wings, ornamental decor made of white metal with a bronze finish, marked "Vve. Tetelin," French. $1,000.00 – 1,200.00.

Plate 49. Clock, 27½"l overall, reclining musician, patinated metal and composition ivory, marble base, French. $1,000.00 – 1,200.00.

Plate 50. Clock, 19½"l, 16"h overall, French, marked "B. Davis, Poitiers," white onyx with gray and black marble inlaid work, decorated with bronze finished metal figures of a woman beckoning a cat. The large numbers on the face are sharply angled, and the clock's body is shaped like an Egyptian headdress. $1,200.00 – 1,400.00.

Plate 51. Mantel Clock, marble, French, clock face marked "Ucra." $275.00 – 325.00.

Plate 52. Clock Set, gray and rose marble with a shape-on-shape design incorporating a diamond, circle, fan, and rectangle: Clock, 13"l, 8½"h; Side Panels, 7"l, 5"h, French. $500.00 – 600.00.

Plate 53. Mantel Set: Clock with matching side vases, marble with ormolu decor, French. $600.00 – 700.00.

Plate 54. Golden Hour Electric Clock, 7½"d, brass base and rim with face of clear glass; manufactured by Jefferson Electric Co., Bellwood, Illinois. $150.00 – 175.00.

Plate 55. Digital Clock, 19"l, bronze, manufactured by Silvercrest, American, ca. mid 1930s. $225.00 – 250.00.

Plate 56. Electric Clock fitted with candle lights, brass and onyx, marked "Silvox," Paris, ca. 1930s. $200.00 – 250.00.

Plate 57. Desk Clock, 4½"h, pot metal base, brass finish, triangle and stepped designs; octagonal shaped clock face, brass. The clock's base is also a bank with coin slot on reverse side. $100.00 – 125.00.

Plate 58. Desk Clock, 5½"l, 4"h, bronze with black enamel trim, marked "JAZ," French, ca. 1930s. $225.00 – 275.00.

Plate 59. Desk Clock, 8½"h, bronze with sterling silver decorative trim, marked with insignia of the Heintz Art Metal Company of Buffalo, New York; 1912 patent date; works by Lux Clock Manufacturing, Waterbury, Connecticut. $200.00 – 225.00.

Plate 60. Westclock "Moonbeam" Clock, 5½" x 6½", celluloid; clock will "flash" rather than sound alarm if desired. $70.00 – 85.00.

Plate 61. Cunningham Alarm Clock, chrome case. $20.00 – 35.00.

Plate 62. Boudoir Clock, 7"h, 6"d, peach colored glass, mirrored base, American. $225.00 – 275.00.

Plate 63. Boudoir or Vanity Clock, plastic base with circular blue glass frame, marked "Teletron," American. $250.00 – 300.00.

Plate 64. Mantel or Shelf Clock, 10"l, 11½"h, ceramic, green glaze, chrome trim, figural dog painted gold sits on top of clock, unmarked. $125.00 – 150.00.

Plate 65. Mantel or Shelf Clock, 12"l, 7"h, ceramic, diamond and stepped fan shapes, marked "St. Clements, France." ca. 1925. $175.00 – 225.00.

Plate 66. Clock, 11" x 7", black painted wood and metal grill screen with brass trim; marked "Onyx NY" with a 1938 patent date. $75.00 – 90.00.

Plate 67. Shelf Clock, 8"h x 10"w, black painted wood and glass combined with clear glass incorporating several deco designs. $20.00 – 30.00.

Plate 68. Lawson Electric Clock designed by Kem Weber, 7½"l x 3½"w, wood case, digital model, American. $125.00 – 150.00.

Plate 69. Mantel or Shelf Clock, walnut case, Westminster chimes, English. $175.00 – 225.00.

Plate 70. Mantel or Shelf Clock, walnut case, ebony trim, marked "British-Made." $175.00 – 225.00.

Plate 71. Mantel Clock, 14½"l, 8¼"h, mahogany and walnut case with inlaid trim and numbers, German. $450.00 – 550.00.

Plate 72. Mantel Clock, mahogany case, 13"h, 28"l, French, ca. 1920s. $600.00 – 700.00.

Dress Accessories

Style and fashion were an important part of the Deco era. Styles changed drastically for women, reflecting a more practical and carefree or casual attitude toward life. The clothing from the Deco years chronicles that transition. The long, corseted gowns of the late Victorian period changed to the knee length skirt and flat chested boyish look of the 1920s. Padded shoulders, tight skirts, and baggy trousers followed in the late 1930s and 1940s. Although there were changes in men's clothing, styles remained conservative compared to the trends which came about with women's apparel.

Although time has been unkind to old garments, vintage Deco clothing is collectible, and there are dealers who specialize in fine examples salvaged from the period. Markets for this type of clothing are usually commercial or public, sold for store displays, museum exhibits, or theatrical production rather than for individual use. But dresses, suits, and coats made from the 1920s through the 1940s currently attract some of the teen and college age generations who enjoy actually wearing the outfits. Estate sales and thrift shops may yield some amusing examples at nominal prices.

While it may be difficult to find a piece of Deco clothing which one would care to wear, a number of items used to accessorize such clothing can be worn with enjoyment. Purses, compacts, belt buckles, dress clips, and all types of jewelry are quite compatible with today's fashion. Dress accessories offer the collector an intriguing and almost unending source of Deco designs. It is apparent from the items shown, as is true for most surveys of the era, that dress accessories were primarily confined to women's articles. But cuff links, stickpins, and watches, for example, were made in Deco styles for men.

Compacts are a product of the Deco age. These neat items made for checking or repairing one's make-up, slipped easily into a purse or evening bag. While most contained a bit of mirror and a cake of powder, some were made with lipstick cases, change holders, and money clips as well. The most expensive are made of gold and silver, but lower priced varieties made of plated or enameled metals and celluloid or plastic are also available. Although small in size, compacts exhibit striking Deco traits. Notice the Egyptian influence on two examples, one with hierglyphics and one with Egyptian figures.

Mesh evening bags made from enameled metals by American manufacturers such as Whiting and Davis were in demand during the 1920s. Small beaded and fringed bags were also popular accessories for the jazz age costume. Evening bags have become a special topic of collector interest and there are few bargains to be found.

Collections of compacts and evening bags can be framed or housed in glass cases to add attractive touches to a room. The same can also be done for much less money with buttons or belt and shoe buckles. These little adornments are sometimes overlooked, but they often created the Deco accent for a garment. Such pieces usually outlived the clothing and many have been saved. Rummage through a box of old buttons and buckles, a Deco souvenir may be found — even a pair of fancy garters!

Jewelry is undoubtedly the most fascinating of all dress accessories. Although gold, silver, and precious stones were fashioned into Deco designs, costume jewelry was born and thrived during those years. Many pieces were made from glass, enameled metals, Bakelite, celluloid, and plastic. Rhinestones, like other good pieces of Deco costume jewelry, are attracting wide interest today. It is obvious that Deco designs have had a great influence on contemporary costume pieces. Reproductions also are surfacing on antique and collectible markets. Buyers should inspect jewelry carefully to determine if an item is new. Prices for authentic period pieces are often comparable with those of good quality modern costume jewelry. (For an excellent study of Art Deco jewelry, see Lillian Baker's *Art Nouveau and Art Deco Jewelry*.)

The Dress Accessories shown here are presented in basically four groups: Beaded and Mesh Bags; Belt Buckles; Compacts; and assorted Jewelry. A few unique items such as a large decorative comb and a pair of beaded garters are also interspersed among those groups!

Plate 73. Beaded Bag, 11"l, Czecho-slovakian glass beads in orange, gold, and black. $125.00 – 150.00.

Plate 74. Mesh Bag, 5½"l x 4¼"w, mul-ticolored abstract design, American. $225.00 – 250.00.

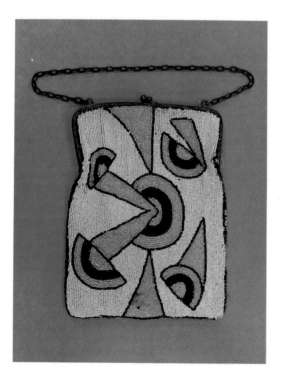

Plate 75. Beaded Bag, 8"l x 6¼"w, black, pink, and green beads form geometric shapes on a background of white beads, American. $150.00 - 175.00.

Plate 76. Beaded Bag, 11"l x 6"w, multi-colored beads compose a design of a large basket of flowers with two Oriental figures on either side, American. $375.00 – 400.00.

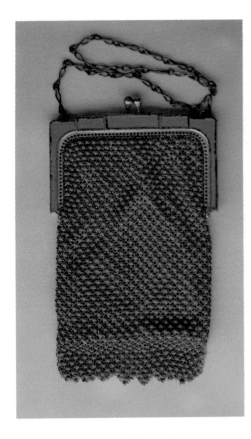

Plate 78. Whiting & Davis Mesh Bag
decorated with a blue, orange, and
black geometric design, American.
$175.00 – 200.00.

Plate 77. Evening Bag, deep orange
enameled mesh, made by Whiting
and Davis, New York, ca. early
1920s. $125.00 – 150.00.

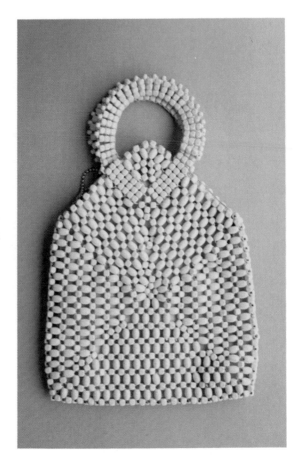

Plate 79. Handbag, large white plastic beads fashioned in a pentagon
shape. $35.00 – 45.00.

Plate 80. Celluloid Purse, 5"l x 3"w, decorated with painted flowers and accented with a scalloped band of rhinestones across the front. $120.00 – 140.00.

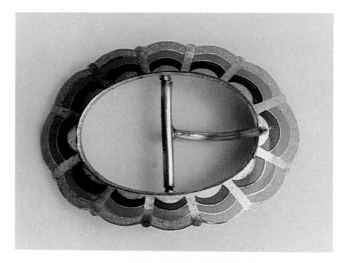

Plate 81. Belt Buckle, repetitive half-moon or crescent enameled designs in shades of green, gold trim, German. $20.00 – 25.00.

Plate 82. Plastic Belt Buckle with two bands of rhinestones, unmarked. $15.00 – 20.00.

Plate 83. Belt Buckles representing a variety of Deco shapes. The center one is made of tortoise shell and the others are plastic. $25.00 – 40.00 each.

Plate 84. Belt Buckle, multicolored Bakelite. $50.00 – 60.00.

Plate 85. Comb, 12"h x11"w, tortoise-shell colored plastic incorporating an elaborate open work design; the unusually large size of this comb makes it an expensive adornment unmarked. $225.00 – 250.00.

Plate 86. Compact, yellow and black enamel, Egyptian figural decor shows the King Tut influence, French. $200.00 – 225.00.

Plate 87. Compact, 2¾"d, brass and red enamel decorated with the figure of a girl in a blue dress and hat, American. $100.00 – 125.00.

Plate 88. Three French Compacts, each featuring young women in various styles of fashion and incorporating glitter work as part of the decor: top, 2½"d, $200.00 – 225.00; left, 1½"d, $175.00 – 200.00; right, $225.00 – 250.00.

Plate 90. Compact, 2¾"d, stainless steel, German. $35.00 – 45.00.

Plate 89. Compact, navy plastic decorated with hand-painted silver bar and wave lines, marked "France." $175.00 – 200.00.

Plate 91. Group of Compacts: Top, silver case covered with black enamel, gold hierglyphics in center. $175.00 – 200.00. Left, black and red enamel in a juxtaposed design, French. $70.00 – 80.00. Right, gold-plated case with black enameled bands, marked "Distributed by Lucien Lelong, New York-Chicago." $70.00 – 80.00.

Plate 92. Volupté Compact, 2¾"sq., light blue enamel with 24 karat gold plate decorated with pink roses, American. $225.00 – 250.00.

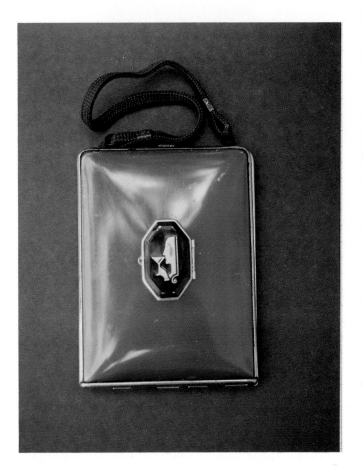

Plate 93. Compact, 4"l x 3"w, red enameled copper featuring a decorative medallion of the profile of a woman drinking from a champagne glass. This compact is fitted with compartments for lip rouge, powder, change, and cigarettes. It has a brown leather strap, marked "Mondaine, New York, U. S. A." $150.00 – 175.00.

Plate 94. Compact in original box (Richard Hudnut, New York, Paris, printed in top), silver case decorated with black and white enamel. $200.00 – 225.00.

Plate 95. Compact, octagonal shape, brass plated, decorated with silver and black tangential designs on green enamel, marked "Richard Hudnut." $100.00 – 175.00.

Plate 96. Compact, German silver, patented 1925. The transition from Art Nouveau is visible in the Deco shape and sunburst ribbing combined with the Nouveau mythical winged images and delicate floral decor. $150.00 – 175.00.

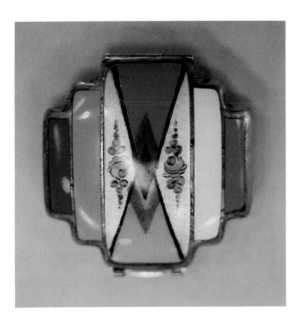

Plate 97. Compact, multicolored enamel decorated with roses, brass plated trim. $175.00 – 200.00.

Plate 98. Compact, gold plated, fitted with a lipstick case. The compact slips into a black file carrying case (not shown), marked "Elgin, U. S. A." $175.00 – 200.00.

Plate 99. Compact on chain with matching lipstick case; lavender enamel decorated with pink roses and blue flowers, octagonal shape, unmarked except for "patent pending," American. $425.00 – 450.00.

Plate 100. Lipstick cases, 2"l, plated silver with silk cords and tassels. $65.00 – 75.00 each.

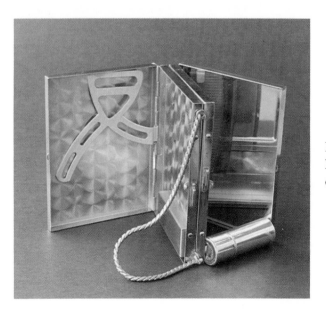

Plate 101. Compact, gold plated, fitted with a lipstick case (left), money clip (right), and chain. $150.00 – 175.00.

Plate 103. Sterling silver Compact, 1½"d; the compact opens on each end and is fitted with a chain, American. $250.00 – 275.00.

Plate 102. Evans Compact with ring and chain, enameled metal with a dark and light blue floral design highlighted by geometric shapes. $250.00 – 275.00.

Plate 104. Compact, silver plated, "1929" engraved on front, unmarked. $150.00 – 175.00.

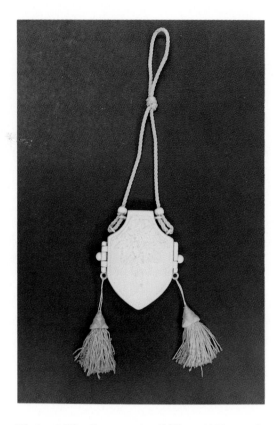

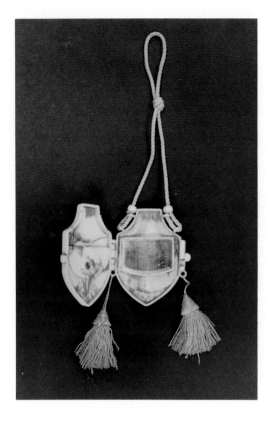

Plate 105. Compact, 4¾"l x 4¼"w, celluloid composition called "French Ivory," pre-1920s, fitted with a silk cord and tassels. $625.00 – 675.00.

Plate 106. Interior of compact in preceding photograph.

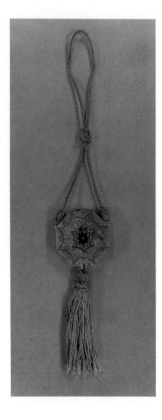

Plate 107. Compact, 2½"d, green celluloid with matching silk cord and tassel, octagonal shape. $325.00 – 375.00.

Plate 108. Compact, 2¼"d, silver metal with a light blue enamel medallion decorated with white roses; fitted with a bracelet style chain, American. $200.00 – 225.00.

Plate 109. Wrist Pact or Watch style Compact, 1¼"d, metal with a silver finish. $150.00 – 175.00.

Plate 110. Telephone Dial Compact, 3¼"d, by Pilcher. The compact is monogrammed with "Willie 8-1759" (perhaps this was a gift from a gentleman who wanted to be sure the lady did not forget his phone number!), American. $250.00 – 275.00.

Plate 111. Bracelet Compact, 3"d, green Bakelite; the center slides open to reveal compartments for rouge and powder; marked "La Parisienne." $400.00 – 450.00.

Plate 112. Interior of Bracelet Compact in preceding photograph.

Plate 113. Beaded Garters, pink and white beads with butterfly wings. $35.00 – 45.00 pair.

Plate 114. Bakelite Bracelet, chunky style composed of multicolored geometric shapes. $200.00 – 225.00.

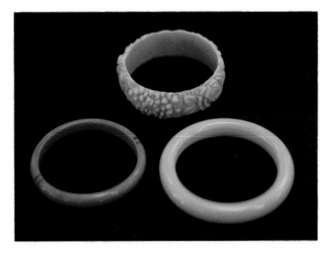

Plate 116. Three Bakelite Bracelets: Top, ivory color with carved floral design. $70.00 – 85.00. Left, slender brown colored ring with a pair of simple incisions on each side. $60.00 – 75.00. Right, smooth ring style in an ivory color. $60.00 – 75.00.

Plate 115. Bakelite Bracelet, jade green, design incorporates deep incisions to form pattern. $100.00 – 120.00.

Plate 117. Bakelite Bracelet, orange and gold marbled color, square shape. $60.00 – 75.00.

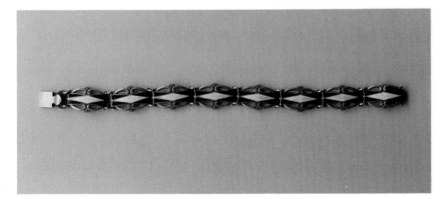

Plate 118. Bracelet, sterling silver, black and green enameled work set in elongated diamond shapes, ca. 1920s. $100.00 – 125.00.

Plate 119. Bracelet, black plastic, set with two large rhinestones. $35.00 – 45.00.

Plate 120. Eisenberg jewelry creations, ca. 1920s: Top, rhinestone Bracelet, double row of alternating rectangular and circular stones. $175.00 – 225.00. Left, Pin, gold Cupid with stylized rhinestone wings. $225.00 – 250.00. Right, rhinestone Pin, overlapping geometric shapes with pavé set stones frame large round stones. $125.00 – 150.00.

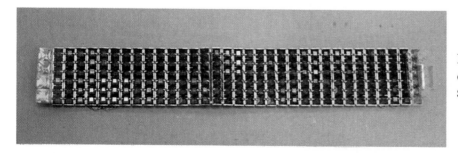

Plate 121. Bracelet, red Czechoslovakian crystals and rhinestones, gold wash. $150.00 – 175.00.

Plate 122. Cuff Links, marbled green Bakelite.
$60.00 – 75.00.

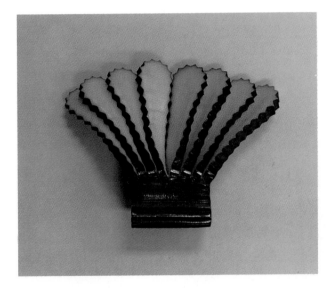

Plate 123. Dress Clip, fan shape in black and
white Bakelite. $50.00 – 60.00.

Plate 124. Dress Clip, black Bakelite, stylized
leaf design. $30.00 – 40.00.

Plate 125. Dress Clip, black Bakelite with an
abstract carved design. $35.00 – 45.00.

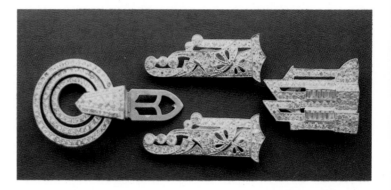

Plate 127. Dress Clips, three different Deco designs of rhinestones in pavé settings. $100.00 – 120.00 each.

Plate 126. Dress Clips: Left, blue rhinestones and turquoise beads, $35.00 – 45.00; right, multicolored rhinestones, $40.00 – 50.00.

Plate 128. Cameos, black Bakelite on clear plastic geometric shapes: Left, rectangle, $70.00 – 80.00; middle, round, $75.00 – 85.00; right, square, $65.00 – 75.00.

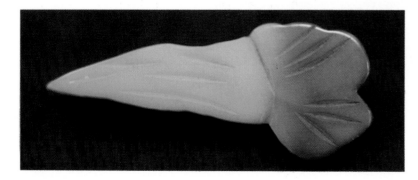

Plate 129. Dress Pin, natural ivory colored Bakelite, abstract design. $35.00 – 45.00.

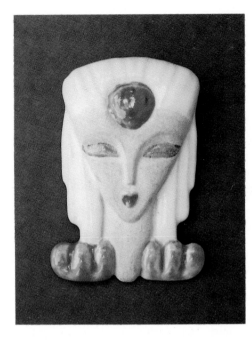

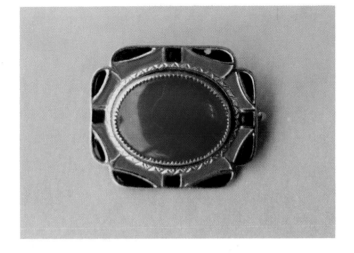

Plate 131. Dress Pin, elliptical green stone set in black and turquoise enamel, silver trim. $35.00 – 45.00.

Plate 130. Dress Pin, ceramic, designed as the face of an Egyptian woman, marked "Seram Art Sculpture by Beth," American. $110.00 – 135.00.

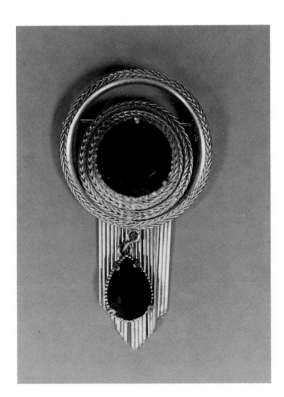

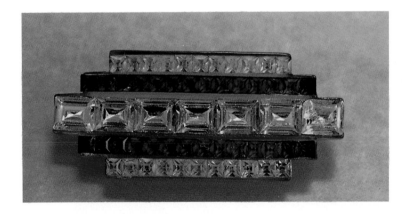

Plate 133. Dress Pin, alternating bars of rhinestones and green glass stones. $100.00 – 120.00.

Plate 132. Dress Pin, gold finished metal set with black onyx stones, marked "Florenza." $100.00 – 125.00.

Plate 134. Dress Pin, large round and rectangular rhinestones set in square design. $60.00 – 75.00.

Plate 135. Dress Pin, large green glass stones surrounded by rhinestones in a four leaf clover design. $50.00 – 60.00.

Plate 136. Dress Pin, large amber glass stones studded with round crystals. $70.00 – 85.00.

Plate 137. Dress Pin, large pink teardrop-shaped crystals accented with round white crystals. $45.00 – 65.00.

Plate 138. Dress Pin, large square cut blue glass stones and goldplated metal fashioned into stylized floral design. $40.00 – 50.00.

Plate 139. Dress Pin, sterling silver, 3"l, figural tennis player, exhibiting bobbed hair and short skirt costume. $60.00 – 70.00.

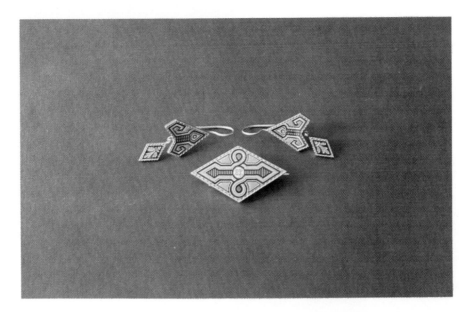

Plate 140. Dress Pin and Earrings, 14k gold, black enamel; pin studded with a small diamond. $1,200.00 – 1,400.00 set.

Plate 141. Ear Clip and Brooch set fashioned of multicolored rhinestones in abstract geometric form. $100.00 – 120.00 set.

Plate 142. Earrings, amber colored glass and clear rhinestones. $50.00 – 65.00 pair.

Plate 143. Earrings, crescent moon shape, black Bakelite with small pearls. $40.00 – 50.00 pair.

Plate 144. Necklace, orange and clear plastic cubes alternating with black beads. $15.00 – 18.00.

Plate 145. Bakelite Necklaces and Bracelet: Top, Bakelite and silver beads. $275.00 – 300.00. Middle, large Bakelite squares separated by small Bakelite beads. $225.00 – 250.00. Bottom, Bakelite bracelet with silver beads matching necklace at top. $125.00 – 150.00.

Plate 146. Necklace, small brass medallions with a square knot design in relief, linked with a small chain, German. $35.00 – 45.00.

Plate 147. Beads, elongated pink art glass beads separated by round burnished gold metal beads. $80.00 – 100.00.

Plate 148. Necklace, rhinestones set in large "V" shape, sterling silver chain. $145.00 – 165.00.

Plate 150. Necklace, rhinestones with a cascade-shaped pendant. $150.00 – 165.00.

Plate 149. Necklace, Venetian glass, large green stones alternate with small clear stones. $120.00 – 135.00.

Plate 151. Beads, gold crystals in geometric shapes. $50.00 – 65.00.

Plate 152. Beads, three sets in various designs in black and white. $65.00 – 75.00 each set.

Plate 153. Necklace, Bracelet, and Ring, 14K white gold filigree combined with French crystals cut with intaglio rays; a small diamond stud in the center of each piece, $1,800.00 – 2,000.00 set.

Plate 154. Watch Pendant, 1¼"l, pentagon shape, green and black enamel, sterling silver trim; back (not shown) decorated with a vertical band of stylized flowers, marked "Borel." $275.00 – 300.00.

Dresser Accessories

Assorted grooming tools can be grouped under the category of dresser accessories simply because the dressing table or vanity is where they were usually kept. This category offers not only variety but also a plentiful supply of Art Deco collectibles. Like dress accessories, men's dresser item are few in number compared to women's. Comb and brush sets, cuff link boxes, and shaving mugs may be found, however.

During Victorian times, the dresser set was in vogue, A set basically consisted of a tray with a matching powder box and hair receiver. Other pieces such as a patch box, pin box, ring tree, talcum shaker, and even a chamber stick were sometimes included. The sets were usually made of porcelain, glass, or silver. Their popularity carried over into the Deco era, although ring trees and hair receivers seem to have diminished popularity during the latter years.

Shapes and decoration of dresser sets gradually began to reflect the changing trends in designs. The floral and fanciful Art Nouveau decor of the late 1890s gave way to streamlined and geometric stylized designs in glass and silver. Porcelain sets began to have more vivid hand-painted decoration, often with sharply contrasting colors. Deco dresser sets were also made in celluloid, or French ivory, as it was sometimes called. Hand mirrors, manicure tools, and even perfume bottles were made to complement the celluloid sets.

Powder boxes, which might also double as small trinket boxes, are the most collectible items from the complete dresser sets. While it may be difficult to find all the matching pieces of an original set, surviving boxes are quite numerous. They were made in so many different sizes and with such diverse decorations that the search for a different one does not become boring. Collections can be easily and attractively displayed. Some of the boxes made during the Deco years were decorated with a nude or semi-nude figure on the lid. Others were even shaped as a figural box as shown in one example here. Powder boxes, like figural bookends, offer an opportunity to acquire a Deco figure for considerably less than a statue or figurine. The original cardboard containers for powder are also collectible, as are other cardboard cosmetic boxes. A few examples have been included. While much less expensive than the glass,

metal, or pottery powder boxes, the cardboard boxes sell for many times over their original price, and empty as well!

Other dresser accessories include combs, clothes brushes, hair brushes, jewelry boxes, and perfume bottles. Collector interest in perfume bottles rivals or surpasses interest in powder boxes. Some of the famous European glass manufacturers of the period such as Lalique, Baccarat, and Moser designed bottles with sharp Deco styles for perfumes and colognes made by various cosmetic firms. Today those original bottles are quite expensive, but others made by American glass companies, often unmarked and thus not attributable to a certain firm, are affordable. Even colognes sold in dime stores at the time which were bottled in Deco style containers or in dark blue, green, or red glass are snapped up by collectors today.

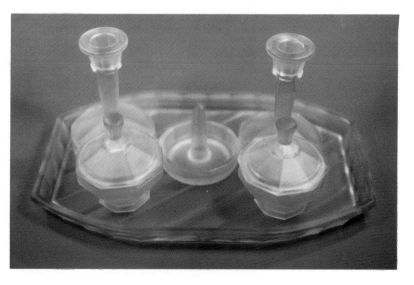

Plate 155. Dresser Set, blue satin glass: Tray, 12"l, Ring Tree, 3"h, two Covered Boxes, 3½"d, two Candleholders, 4½"h; Depression era, American. $125.00 –150.00 set.

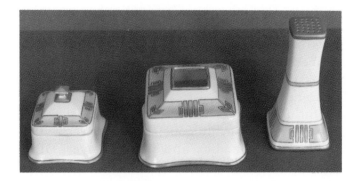

Plate 156. Dresser Set, porcelain, Limoges, France; blanks with hand-painted American decoration; blue and gold geometric shapes outlined with red. Dresser Tray, 16"l, pierced "butterfly" handles. $250.00 – 300.00 set.

Plate 157. Matching pieces to Dresser Set in preceding photograph: Pin Box, Hair Receiver, and Talcum Shaker.

Plate 158. Dresser Set, porcelain with silver and blue hand-painted trim, Czechoslovakian; Candleholders, Powder Box, and Pin Box. $125.00 – 150.00 set.

Plate 159. Chamberstick, 6"h, porcelain; multicolored stylized birds and geometric patterns, hand painted; Noritake China Company, Japan. $100.00 – 125.00.

Plate 160. Lucite beveled Hand Mirror. $25.00 – 35.00.

Plate 161. Matching Hand Mirror, Comb, Hair Brush, and Powder Box; celluloid with black and gray geometric designs and stylized floral decoration. $200.00 – 250.00 set.

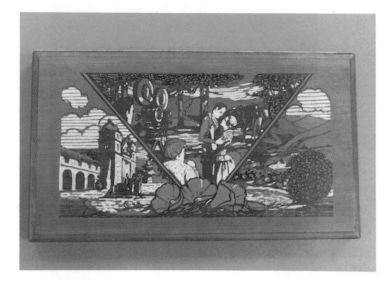

Plate 162. Trinket or Souvenir Box, 16½"l x 9¼"w, wood, decorated with a hand-painted movie scene on cover, American, ca. 1930s–1940s. $100.00 – 120.00.

Plate 163. Pin Tray, 7"l, nude figure incorporated into design, pink glass, American. $50.00 – 65.00.

Plate 164. Jewel Box, Limoges porcelain, octagonal shape, hand-painted abstract design, French. $225.00 – 275.00.

Plate 165. Jewel Box, ceramic; black, green, and yellow enameled abstract designs, brass trim, marked "Boch Frères, Made in Belgium," artist signed, "A. Louviers." $275.00 – 325.00.

Plate 166. Jewel Box, 2½"h x 6½"l, nickel silver, interior lined with black velvet. $30.00 – 40.00.

Plate 167. Dresser Box, 6½"l, pink glass base fitted with compartments; gilded metal lid with figure of a ballet dancer on top. $225.00 – 250.00 (mc).

Plate 168. Jewel Box, 8" x 5", brass, painted red and black with lid cut to form geometric and checkered designs. $65.00 – 75.00.

Plate 169. Powder Box, 3½"d, "Windsor Diamond" pattern, clear glass, made by Jeanette Glass Company, ca. late 1930s, American. $40.00 – 50.00.

Plate 170. Dresser Box, 5"w x 2½"h, green and black Bakelite, knob feet. $80.00 – 100.00.

Plate 171. Powder Box, chrome with white plastic and ebony heart shapes on lid, glass insert, Chase (called an "Occasional Box" in the company catalog). $75.00 – 90.00.

Plate 172. Powder Box, ceramic, bold abstract decoration hand painted in vivid colors, black trim, artist signed, marked "Made in Czechoslovakia." $80.00 – 100.00.

Plate 173. Powder Box, 5½"h, chrome, decorated with three shades of green enamel, fitted with a glass insert for powder, mirror inside lid. $75.00 – 90.00.

Plate 174. Powder Box, 8½"h, frosted glass, semi-nude figural shape, unmarked. $75.00 – 100.00.

Plate 175. Powder Box, light green glass; a pair of figural nudes ("Twins") sit on top of lid, American. $120.00 – 140.00.

Plate 176. Powder Box, 3½"h, 5"d, marble adorned with 5½"h enameled pot-metal figure in huntress attire, ivory face, unmarked. $275.00 – 325.00.

Plate 177. Powder Box, ceramic, decorated with a dancing nude figure holding a drape, German. $75.00 – 100.00.

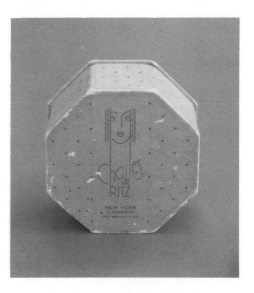

Plate 178. Charles of the Ritz Face Powder Box. $10.00 – 15.00.

Plate 179. Assortment of Cosmetic Boxes: Left, Jonteel Cold Cream, American. $25.00 – 30.00. Upper middle, Princess Pat Week End Set (contained assorted items). $70.00 – 75.00. Right, Love Me Face Powder, Chicago, Melba Mfg. $50.00 – 60.00. Lower middle, *Poudre* (powder), Paris, $55.00 – 65.00.

Plate 180. Cologne Boxes: Top, floral cover, "Cara Nome" printed on front. $15.00 – 20.00. Bottom, Dorothy Perkins "Lilac" Cologne. $20.00 – 25.00.

Plate 181. "Kares" Dresser Items in box originally containing face powder, rouge, perfume, and talcum powder, marked "Woolworth, Paris, New York." $275.00 – 300.00.

Plate 182. Perfume Bottles in gold fitted case, clear glass with gold-plated tops, marked "Lucien Lelong." $100.00 – 120.00.

Plate 183. Perfume Bottles, 1½"d, triangle and hexagon shapes made of sterling silver and onyx. $80.00 – 100.00 each.

Plate 184. DeVilbiss double Perfume Bottles, 2"h, in box, marked with manufacturer's name and "Toledo U. S. A." $275.00 – 300.00.

Plate 185. Ronson "PerFu-Mist," Refillable Perfume Dispensers for a woman's purse. $100.00 – 125.00 each.

Plate 186. Perfume Bottle, 3"h, black glass decorated with a silver lattice work border, French. $140.00 – 160.00.

Plate 187. Perfume Bottle, 6½"h, black glass decorated in gold with the figures of a woman and child, French; designed by Iribe for Lanvin, ca. 1927. $175.00 – 200.00.

Plate 188. Perfume Bottle (left) and Powder Jar (right), 5¼" h, amber glass; spherical bodies with cube-shaped tops, signed "Moser," Karlsbad, Bohemia. $600.00 – 700.00 pair.

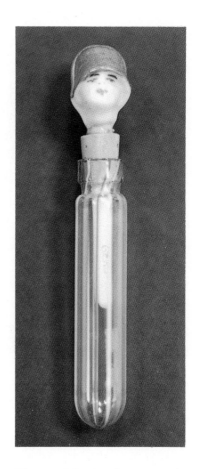

Plate 189. Perfume Vial, 3¼" h, glass with a ceramic head of a woman wearing a hat serving as the stopper, German. $100.00 – 125.00.

Plate 190. Perfume Vials in animal forms, glass, German: left, Cat, $85.00 – 95.00; right, Dog, ca. 1920s. $110.00 – 125.00.

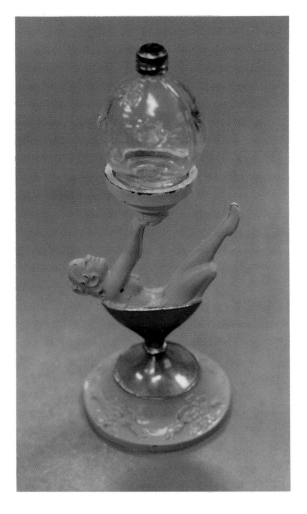

Plate 192. Perfume Atomizer, 7"h, amber and black glass, French, ca. 1920s. $275.00 – 300.00.

Plate 191. Perfume Bottle held aloft by nude woman in a tub, pedestal base, painted metal, made by Sculptor Products Co., American, ca 1920s. $350.00 – 375.00 (mc).

Plate 193. Perfume Atomizer, 5¾"h, yellow satin glass with enameled flowers, black accents, French, ca. 1920s. $300.00 – 325.00.

Plate 195. Shaving Brush, green marbled Bakelite. $25.00 – 35.00.

Plate 194. Perfume Lamp, 7", orange glass with a satin finish, stepped design, unmarked, ca. 1920s. $350.00 – 375.00.

Plate 196. Razor Bank, porcelain, shaped in the form of a Scottie, Japanese. $35.00 – 45.00.

Plate 197. Hair Brush, brown plastic, stepped design. $20.00 – 25.00.

Plate 198. Man's Brush and Comb Set in fitted case, monogrammed, nickel silver. $70.00 – 95.00 set.

Plate 199. EverReady Night Light, 4¼"h, hammered metal finish decorated with chrome bands. $35.00 – 45.00.

Plate 200. Vanity Mirror on faux marble vase with pot-metal figure of a nude posed in dance position. $225.00 – 250.00 (mc).

Plate 201. Towel Bar, extension style, from 5½" to 7½", ship motif with intricate stylized base forms back mount, brass. $150.00 – 175.00.

Plate 202. Pieces to a Wash Set: Bowl and Pitcher Set with Toothbrush Holder, red and black abstract pattern, European. $400.00 – 450.00 set.

Plate 203. Wash Bowl, 12½"d, and Pitcher, 9½"h, ceramic, "Rose Marie" pattern, hand-painted black and rose geometric decor, made by the Keller and Guerin Pottery, French. $300.00 – 350.00 set.

Lamps and Light Fixtures

Electricity was available to many American homes during the years between the First and Second World Wars. Electric lamps became an important part of the home furnishings market. Businesses such as department stores, offices, restaurants, and theaters were another large sector of the economy in need of modern forms of light fixtures. Lighting manufacturers catered to both markets, parlaying topical Deco themes into various forms of light.

Floor lamps and table top lamps are both quite collectible. Selections may be elegant and high style or simply low camp and amusing. Lamps are not only ingenious relics of Deco design but they are also functional. Collectors should check the electrical wiring, however. Many still have the original cords which may be frayed or split, but rewiring is not too expensive. It is well worth the effort to have lamps repaired so that they can be displayed to full advantage. Rewiring does not detract but rather adds to the lamp's value.

Floor lamps supported widely flared shades or globes. These reflected the light upward and torchère has become the name associated with that particular style. The shades were made of frosted or opaque glass or out of metal such as brass or chrome. This same type of lamp is now frequently reproduced to complement new Deco-style furniture. Other Deco floor lamps had conventional parchment or silk shades with the "modern" look showing up in the stems and bases.

Figural table lamps are very much in demand. Both French and American companies made numerous varieties aimed at the middle class market. Women, nude or semi-nude, were fashioned in various stylized poses such as dancing, kneeling, or with arms stretched high in the air. The light globe was positioned to the side or behind the figure or even rested in the figure's hands. These lamps were decorative objects, designed to cleverly disguise the source of light.

Although this type of figural lamp was made in bronze, most of the ones found today were made of metal alloys. The finish may be bronze colored or painted red, black, green, and so forth. Because the paint wears and chips over time, it is not uncommon for the lamps to be repainted, especially for resale. But lower prices should be reflected if that is the case. Globes on these lamps, because of their fragile nature, often have been replaced as well. It goes without saying that the most desirable lamps are those with all original parts and finish.

Regarding prices, the French figural lamps are the most expensive, and it is not uncommon for these to be near or over $2,000, outside the range for the moderate collector. While American specimens are considerably less costly, it is still rare to find an all original one for less than $250. Those not in working order and needing repairs are about the only ones which might be bargains. The Frankart Company, located in New York City, was probably the most prolific manufacturer of metal figural Deco lamps. Frankart lamps, like their other products, such as bookends, are increasingly popular. Prices have risen so much, that some Frankart examples are almost in a par in price with some French examples.

Ceramic and glass Deco lamps were also made in figural designs. One ceramic lamp shown here, made by the Van Briggle Pottery, is a finely executed piece of American art pottery. Interest in American art pottery in recent years has also resulted in higher prices for such examples. Other ceramic lamps portray a Deco influence by their hand-painted body decor in geometric or stylized configurations. Glass lamps may feature similar Deco characteristics in either the body or the shade as illustrated in some of the photographs. The boudoir lamp with the nude glass globe is an American mass-produced piece imitating the Lalique style.

Deco light fixtures designed for commercial enterprises can be turned into attractive lighting for homes. Torchère or conical-shaped wall sconces adapt to baths, halls, and bedrooms while cascading chandeliers and other large fixtures can be used to light entrance foyers or porches. Shops specializing in architectural antiques may offer some interesting examples. Most commercial fixtures were made of bronze, brass, or even cast iron, and these have survived the years quite well. Shapes are unquestionably Deco!

Plate 204. Lamp, 21"h, semi-nude figure, white metal with silver finish, black marble base, the tambourine serves as a light shade, marked "Fayral," French, ca. mid 1920s. $2,000.00 – 2,200.00.

Plate 205. Boudoir Lamp, pot metal, painted green finish, dancing nude figure, marked "Beaver patent pending," American. (Shade is not original.) $500.00 – 600.00.

Plate 207. Boudoir Lamp, 8½"l, 8"h, pot metal, painted green finish, seated nude figure, amber crackle glass globe, American, marked "Kelly Creations." $600.00 – 700.00.

Plate 206. Lamp, bronzed metal, three kneeling nude figures support tortoise colored glass globe, unmarked. $700.00 – 800.00.

Plate 208. Boudoir Lamp, 8½"h, dancing nude figure, pot metal with bronze finish, marked "Rhythm" on base. When the bulb is turned on behind the splotched painted glass shade there is an illusion of movement, unmarked. $200.00 – 250.00.

Plate 209. Boudoir Lamp, 8"h, pot-metal base incorporates Art Nouveau lines. Frosted glass shade exhibits Deco style with nude figure and molded overlapping half moon designs in corners, unmarked. $225.00 – 275.00.

Plate 211. Pair of Boudoir or Vanity Lamps; white metal with bronze colored finish; nude figures stand in stylized position on right side of holders with flame style bulbs, marked "Frankart." $1,200.00 – 1,400.00 pair.

Plate 210. Lamp, 8½"h x 10½"w, gold crackle glass globe on stepped base with a kneeling nude figure on each side with arms outstretched to support globe; Frankart, Inc., New York City, ca 1920s. $800.00 – 1,000.00.

Plate 212. Table Lamp, 19½"h, porcelain figure dressed in a long gown; elaborate headdress supports the shade, a sphere made of slag glass; burled wood base, Cubist influence, marked "Argilor, Paris." $2,000.00 – 2,400.00.

Plate 213. Aronson Lamp, 13½"h, incorporating an incense burner in the form of a kneeling nude figure, copper finish; base dated "1923," marked "L.V. Aronson, Homeric Bronze." Shade combines silk panels with metal artwork. There is a 1922 date mark on the shade. (L. V. Aronson was the founder of the New Jersey Art Metal Works. Ronson products such as cigarette lighters were also made by his company.) $1,000.00 – 1,200.00.

Plate 214. Table Lamp, ceramic, figural nude base, blue matt glaze, marked "Van Briggle," a Colorado Springs art pottery. $800.00 – 1,000.00.

Plate 215. Table Lamp, 14"h, nude figure sits on top of column with knees bent and head turned to one side; porcelain, bisque finish, chrome base; Lenox, Trenton, New Jersey, ca. 1930s. $400.00 – 450.00.

Plate 216. Table Lamp, brass, slag glass panels and silk fringe enhance octagonal shade, unmarked. $300.00 – 350.00.

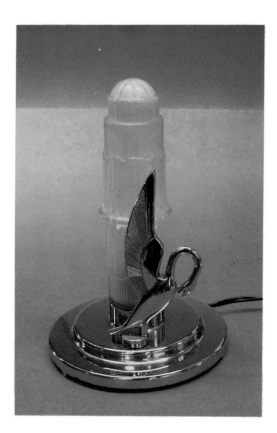

Plate 217. Table Lamp, 10"h, candle style glass shade in holder on round chrome base; the figure of a stylized swan with wing in vertical position is incorporated into the design. $175.00 – 200.00.

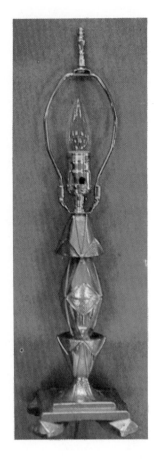

Plate 218. Table Lamp, marked "1928, Armour Bronze Corp," metal alloy with lacquered copper finish; combination of different geometric shapes stacked on a footed stepped base. $140.00 – 160.00.

Plate 219. Table Lamp, 11½"h, glass, represents the planet Saturn, commemorative of the 1939 World's Fair. $325.00 – 375.00.

Plate 221. Ceiling Light Fixture, brass cone shapes with open work hold scalloped fan-shaped frosted glass shades. $250.00 – 350.00.

Plate 220. Table Lamp, 14"h, cascade or waterfall-shaped shade, opalescent glass, marked "Sabino," French. $2,200.00 – 2,500.00.

Plate 222. Wall Sconce, brass, 10"h, typical fixture for theaters, American. $150.00 – 175.00.

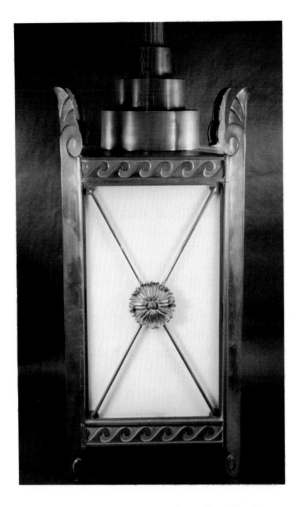

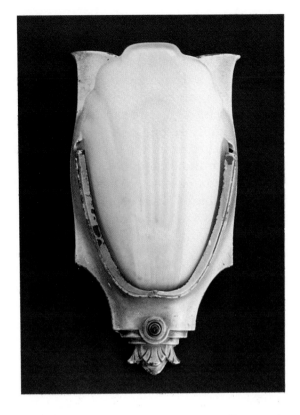

Plate 224. Wall Sconce, painted metal, frosted glass shade with interior painted pink, American. $45.00 – 55.00 (mc).

Plate 223. Commercial Light Fixture, 29½"h, copper and bronze with opaline glass panels. $2,200.00 – 2,400.00.

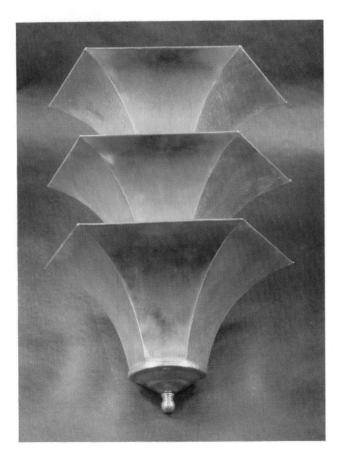

Plate 225. Wall Sconce, 14½"h, chrome, French. $350.00 – 450.00.

Library and Study Accessories

Numerous types of items associated with reading and writing were made along Deco lines. Bookends, ink wells, and desk sets are representative items. Such accessories are expected to be found in a library or study setting and complement its furnishings. These often have a bold or masculine look as well as Deco traits. Additional objects have been included in this category. These could easily be found in the library although one might find them in other rooms as well. For example, radios, electric fans, frames, and wallhangings are shown in this section.

Desk accessories made nice gifts, and it is not unusual to find monograms on such items as letter openers and desk boxes. Most of the sets were made of metal, usually brass, bronze, or silver. Fine jewelry and department stores had desk items made especially for their firms. The company name appeared either alone or with the manufacturer's name on pieces. Expect pieces with such famous names as Cartier or Tiffany to be quite expensive. Desk items made and marked by American metal companies such as Silvercrest, Bronz-Met, and Heintz are usually moderately priced.

Figural bookends are an interesting Deco library accessory. Animal, bird, or human figures can be found. As is the case with most figural pieces, the bookends say "Deco" at a glance. These seem to be the least expensive of any type of figural pieces as indicated by the prices quoted for examples shown here. Figures made into bookends do not require the same amount of workmanship that some other figural combinations do, such as clocks or lamps. Moreover, some of these are two dimensional and stamped from a metal sheet. Collectors searching for an affordable Deco figure will find that bookends offer some good possibilities.

Plate 226. Bookends, 7"h, kneeling nude figures with hands placed on top of shoulder and on side of head, marked "Bronze Art." $275.00 – 325.00 pair.

Plate 227. Bookends, 8"h, nudes with arms stretched overhead, males kneeling at their feet; dark finish, marked "Bronzmet, Pat. July 22, 1924, copyright 1923, Gifthouse, Inc., NYC." $250.00 – 300.00 pair.

Plate 228. Bookends, 8"h, bronze, nudes, each flanked by a pair of greyhounds. The curvilinear arch work enhances the streamlined figures, German, ca. early 1920s. $400.00 – 450.00 pair.

Plate 229. Bookends, 5"h, nudes in dance position; bronze with green finish, stylized floral design on base, marked "Schroedin, Solid Bronze." $300.00 – 350.00 pair.

Plate 230. Bookends, 3¼"h, 4½"w, figural golf players, cast brass, marked "Art Brass Co., N.Y." $300.00 – 350.00 pair.

Plate 231. Indian Head Bookends, 3½"h, 4½"w, cast iron with painted gold finish, unmarked, American. $50.00 – 65.00 (mc).

Plate 232. Bookend, figures of two terriers mounted on base, bronze finish, marked "Fashioned by Ronson," American. $150.00 – 200.00 pair.

Plate 233. Bookends, 7"h, Scottie dogs, metal, brass finish, Frankart, New York City, ca. 1920s. $225.00 – 275.00 pair.

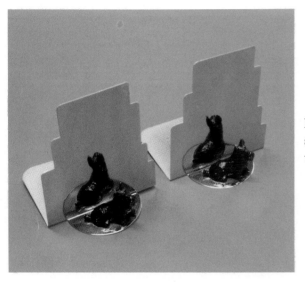

Plate 234. Bookends, 4½"h, chrome, stepped shape with black metal Scotties sitting in front, unmarked. $60.00 – 75.00 pair.

Plate 235. Bookends, 4½"h, cast metal, small figures of horses with a gold finish stand on top of three-level base with a silver-gray finish, unmarked. $175.00 – 225.00 pair.

Plate 236. Bookends, 5½"h, stylized metal figure of a dog on a faux marble base, Frankart. $225.00 – 250.00 pair.

Plate 237. Bookends, 7"h, white porcelain horse heads with gold trim on black bases, European. $175.00 – 225.00 pair.

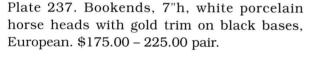

Plate 238. Bookends, 5¼"h, bird or eagle figures fashioned with a sharp angular design, bronze, unmarked. $150.00 – 200.00 pair.

Plate 239. Bookends, 4½"h, sail boats mounted on half-moon shaped base topped with a solid round circle, bronze, marked "NuArt." $125.00 – 150.00 pair.

Plate 240. Bookends, 7"h, sailboats, made by Bronze Art. $175.00 – 225.00 pair.

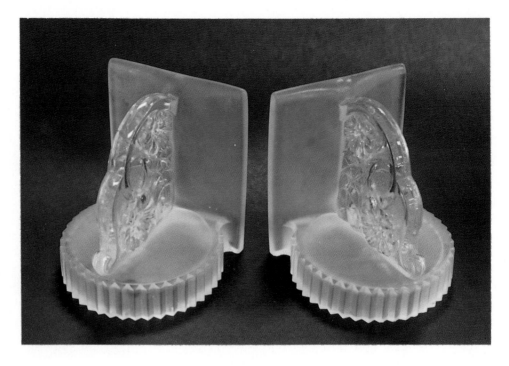

Plate 241. Bookends, 5"h, frosted glass combining three shapes, unmarked, American. $125.00 – 150.00 pair.

Plate 242. Bookend, 6½"h, rose and white marble combined in a geometric configuration. $175.00 – 225.00 pair.

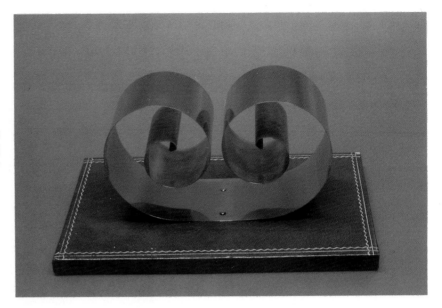

Plate 243. Book Holder, 10½"l, chrome spiral mounted on leather base, labeled "Spring Life, The Automatic Book Rack." $25.00 – 45.00.

Plate 244. Note Pad Holder, 8¼"l, black Bakelite in shape of a Scottie. $60.00 – 75.00.

Plate 245. Newspaper Holder, 11¼"h, 8½"w, metal, copper finish. $45.00 – 55.00.

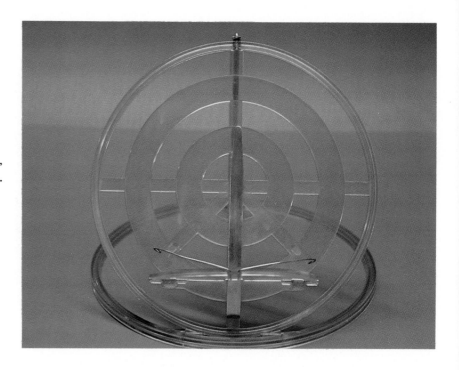

Plate 246. Book Rest, made for a train, folding style, Lucite, 1938 patent date. $125.00 – 150.00.

Plate 247. Letter Holder, 3½"h, 5"w, brass, marked "Bradley & Hubbard," American. $75.00 – 100.00.

Plate 248. Desk Accessories: Calendar and Envelope Holders, bronze, marked "Silvercrest," American. $100.00 – 125.00 set.

Plate 249. Desk Accessories: Inkwell, Letter Holder, and Blotter, brass, unmarked. $200.00 – 250.00 set.

Plate 250. Inkwell and Pen Tray, sterling silver decoration on bronze, made by Heintz Art Metal Company, Buffalo, New York. $450.00 – 500.00 set.

Plate 251. Calendar Holder, Envelope Holder, Blotter Corner, and Letter Opener matching Inkwell and Pen Tray in preceding photograph.

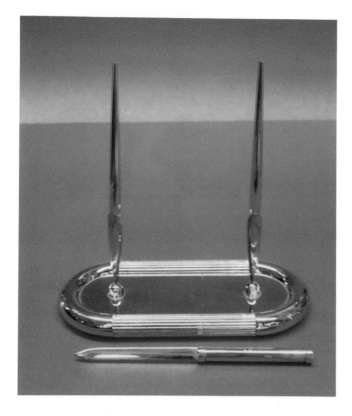

Plate 252. Pen Set with Letter Opener, silver-plate. $200.00 – 225.00 set.

Plate 253. Inkwell, brass, 3½"h, attached tray, 6"l. $120.00 – 140.00.

Plate 254. Inkwell and Pen, 3½"h, black plastic, marked "Morrise Pen-Ink Unit, LA, CA," 1939 patent date. $50.00 – 65.00.

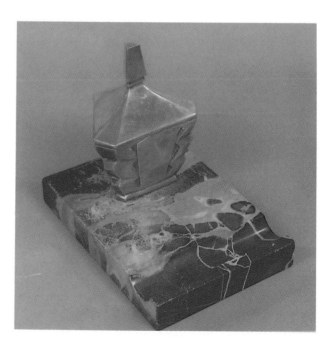

Plate 255. Inkwell, 2¼"h, bronze with silver finish mounted on black marble base, signed "Rischmann," French. $350.00 – 400.00.

Plate 256. Inkwell, hammered copper and cast brass. $150.00 – 175.00.

Plate 257. Picture Frame, chrome with red and cream enameled glass. Frame will hold a 1½" x 2" picture. $30.00 – 40.00.

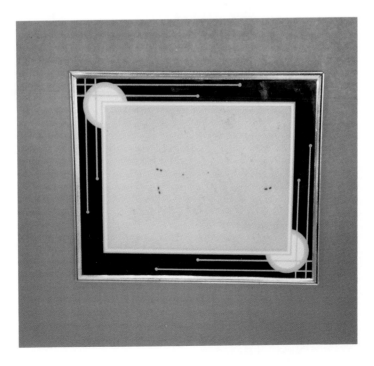

Plate 258. Picture Frame, 10" x 12", abstract silver design on wide black border. $60.00 – 75.00.

Plate 259. Picture Frame, wood and glass. The picture illustrates a suite of bedroom furniture designed by André Domin for the 1925 Paris Exhibition. $70.00 – 85.00 (frame only).

Plate 260. Picture Frame, 12½"l, marble and glass, designed as a double frame, French. $125.00 – 150.00.

Plate 261. Wall Plaques, chrome design of a woman with head resting on shoulder mounted on cobalt blue glass. $60.00 – 75.00 pair.

Plate 262. Magazine Rack, 15½"h, 11"d, nude and frolicking greyhound, bronze with silver finish. $750.00 – 850.00.

Plate 263. Tapestry, Egyptian figures and hierglyphics. $250.00 – 300.00.

Plate 264. Tapestry, 64½"l, Egyptian motif featuring a sphinx, French. $300.00 – 400.00.

Plate 265. Temperature Gauge, plastic, marked "Taylor Humidiguide." $35.00 – 45.00.

Plate 266. Electric Fan, 12"d, marked "Gilbert," brass blades. $175.00 – 200.00.

Plate 267. Ceiling Fan made in the form of an airplane engine and propeller, chrome. $1,300.00 – 1,500.00.

Plate 268. Mah Jong Tiles, Bakelite, in case. $125.00 – 150.00 set.

Plate 269. Radio, 8"h, 11"w, wood and chrome, marked "Fada." $350.00 – 400.00.

Plate 270. Radio, 9"h, 17"l, blue glass and wood, chrome trim, marked "Sparton." $2,000.00 – 2,200.00.

Plate 271. Telephone, candlestick style, 13"h, brass. $250.00 – 275.00.

Plate 272. Grate, 38½"h x 23½"w, wrought iron, abstract geometric and floral designs, marked "Made in France." $400.00 – 500.00.

Plate 273. Door Knockers, 6½"l, brass, Egyptian style designs. $75.00 – 85.00 each.

Smoking Accessories

The cigarette, like the cocktail, became a mark of sophistication, one of the "in" things during the Deco years. To smoke (and drink) showed one was in step with the "modern" world. This was especially true for women as they shed the forbidding Victorian rules dictating "proper" conduct. More and more women began to smoke in public just as they shortened their hemlines and bobbed their hair.

A number of interesting smoker's items were made which were either desirable or necessary accessories for those addicted to the habit. For example, ashtrays were indispensable. Both table top and free standing varieties became common fixtures in the home. Most were made of metals such as brass, copper, bronze, and chrome but glass and ceramic ones were also prevalent. The ever-popular nude figures sometimes were incorporated into the design. Two shown here include a rather simple table top model and an elaborate floor style.

In conjunction with ashtrays, "silent butlers" became an appropriate household item. The name was an apt description for this receptacle fitted with a long handle and hinged lid. For those who had no real butler, these were handy gadgets for emptying overflowing ashtrays at one's party or cleaning up the stale remains the next day! They were usually made of chrome, brass, or frequently hammered aluminum. The latter type, however, do not always fit the Deco image even though they are from the period.

Cigarette holders cover a broad category of smoking collectibles. In fact, the term "holder" can have several different meanings when used in connection with cigarettes. Table top holders refer to open or covered boxes for keeping a convenient supply of cigarettes. These were made as individual containers or as a combination piece with space for cigarettes and matches and even an ashtray. The boxes were also often part of a matching set of separate pieces.

Another type of holder was the cigarette dispenser. These novel items are a good example of the "purely fun" side of the Deco years. One of the dispensers shown is a "pop up" type, operating with a spring device. Cigarettes encased in metal holders pop up when the lid is removed. Another has concealed push buttons on two sides. When pressed, the hinged lid opens, revealing individual spaces for cigarettes. A third type of dispenser has a roll-top. When it is pushed back, a tray slides out offering five cigarettes.

The term cigarette holder, however, is perhaps most commonly associated with the individual holder. While these were designed for keeping the cigarette from direct contact with the mouth, they were also used for effect, to impart a chic or debonair look! The holders shown here range in length from two to twelve inches. They are made of plastic, tortoise shell, or celluloid.

Art Deco cigarette lighters comprise still another group of smoking accessories. Collectors are interested in both the table top and the pocket or purse varieties. Most of the pocket lighters have masculine overtones. Of course, it was the custom for a man to light a woman's cigarette. Two lighters shown here with floral decor appear strictly feminine, however. One, in fact, is a combination compact and cigarette lighter.

The Ronson "bar-tender" lighters are probably the most coveted of the table top models among enthusiasts. Two versions were made (see Cummings, 1992, pp. 148 and 165). One style is shown here. Although they were made as novelties, these rather rare items fetch hundreds of dollars today.

Incense burners are included in this section. They may be used to mask tobacco odors, and they are complementary in a decorative scheme. Other tobacco related Deco collectibles include cigarette and cigar cases, cigar clippers and cutters, pipe stands, tobacco jars, and humidors. Beware that general collectors of tobacciana make the market quite competitive.

Plate 274. Ashtray and Match Holder, 4½"h, metal and glass; nude figure in kneeling position with match holder attached to back on black base with opaque green glass ashtray, unmarked. $250.00 – 300.00.

Plate 275. Ashtray, topped by nude figure with one knee raised and arms stretched behind back, 9½"h, pewter finish, marked "N.S.A. Mfg. Co.,Chicago, Pat. Applied For." $275.00 – 325.00.

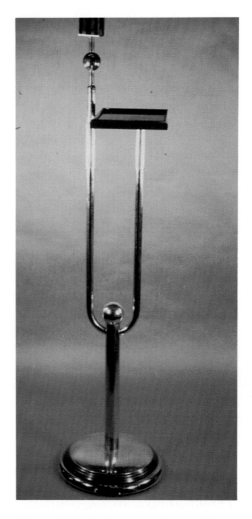

Plate 276. Ashtray, floor model, 35"h, equipped with Match Holder, chrome, black enamel trim. $225.00 – 275.00.

Plate 277. Ashtray, sphere shape with nude figure in standing position with arms behind back 10½"h, metal with green finish, marked "British Made." $300.00 – 350.00.

Plate 278. Ashtray, floor model, nude figure, 24"h, arms stretched overhead to support tray, cast metal, Frankart, New York City, ca. 1920s. $800.00 – 1,000.00.

Plate 279. Ashtray, floor model, 33"h, cast metal, silver finish, stepped designed handle and tray holder with glass insert, marked "Seville Art Studio." $175.00 – 200.00.

Plate 280. Ashtray, ceramic, 4"d, marked "Snufferette, National Porcelain Co., Trenton, N.J." $30.00 – 40.00.

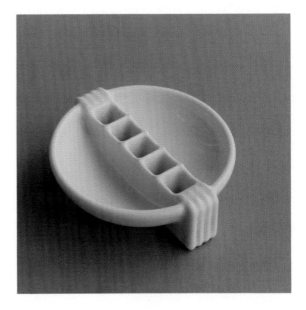

Plate 281. Ashtray, ceramic, cobalt blue glaze, 4½"d, marked "Snufferette, Ekstrand Mfg. Co., Inc., NY, The Executive." $35.00 – 45.00.

Plate 282. Ashtray and Match Holder, ceramic with dark blue glaze; sitting nude figure, 5¼"h, holds ball-shaped ashtray; marked "Made in Japan." $40.00 – 50.00 pair.

Plate 283. Ashtray, ceramic, 6"l, woman's profile fitted with bathing cap, hand painted, Japanese. $25.00 – 30.00.

Plate 284. Bridge Set Ashtrays made in the form of diamonds and hearts, enamel and metal, marked "Con-Den-So." When a lighted cigarette is placed on the channel, it will go out. $80.00 – 90.00 set.

Plate 285. Ashtray, 5"d, dark blue glass decorated with a chrome sailboat, marked "F.D. Co.," American. $50.00 – 60.00.

Plate 286. Ashtrays, 4"d, "Manhattan" pattern Depression glass decorated with suits of playing cards, made by Anchor Hocking Glass Co. of Ohio. $15.00 – 18.00 each.

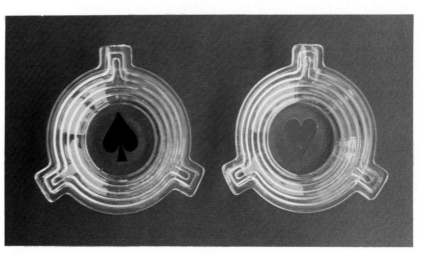

Plate 287. Assortment of black glass ashtrays in several geometric styles, unmarked. Top, $15.00 – 18.00; bottom, 10.00 – 12.00 each.

Plate 288. Figural Ashtray by NuArt; seated nude figure, cast metal painted with a gold finish, holds an amber glass tray, American. $150.00 – 175.00 (mc).

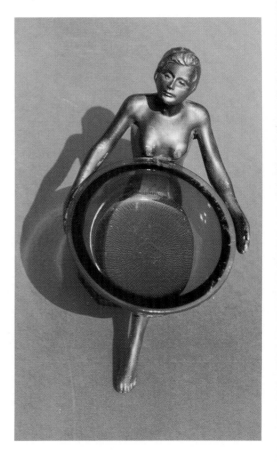

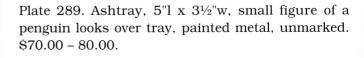

Plate 289. Ashtray, 5"l x 3½"w, small figure of a penguin looks over tray, painted metal, unmarked. $70.00 – 80.00.

Plate 290. Ashtray, 3"h x 5"w, tray is support-ed on the backs of three kneeling nude figures; cast metal with a black finish, unmarked. $100.00 – 120.00.

Plate 291. Ashtray, chrome, open sphere shape with attached section to hold cig-arette, marked "Manning Bowman, Meriden, Conn., U.S.A." $35.00 – 45.00.

Plate 292. Ashtray, 7"l, chrome with black enamel trim. $15.00 – 18.00 (mc).

Plate 293. Ashtray, 6"d, chrome combined with wood and plastic, unmarked. $30.00 – 40.00.

Plate 294. Chase "Aristocrat" Ashtray, 5½"l, chrome. $35.00 – 45.00 (mc).

Plate 295. Ashtrays, chrome: left, 4½"d, figural birds' beaks hold cigarette, marked "Diecasters, Ridgefield, N. J.," $40.00 – 50.00; right, 4"d, vertical holder in middle of tray has individual spaces to hold several cigarettes, unmarked, $35.00 – 45.00.

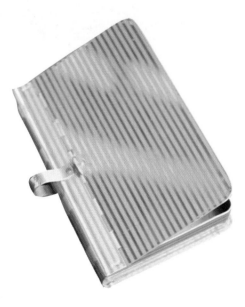

Plate 296. Silent Butler, 9"l, chrome, rectangular with ribbed design on lid, unmarked. $40.00 – 50.00.

Plate 297. Silent Butler, 11⅜" l, chrome with plastic handle, Chase. $65.00 – 80.00.

Plate 299. Smoking Set: Ashtray, Cigarette Holder, and Match holder; Indian symbol motif. $225.00 – 250.00.

Plate 298. This ashtray and the following three photographs are examples of smoking accessories made by the Heintz Art Metal Company of Buffalo, New York. It is marked with the Heintz monogram and "Sterling on Bronze," with a patent date of 1912. This ashtray was part of a nested set made for the B. Altman Company. The Heintz pieces all have various stylized geometric designs in sterling silver. $35.00 – 50.00 set.

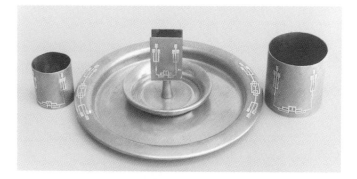

Plate 300. Smoking Set: left, Match Holder; center, Tray, 10"d with Ashtray and book style Match Holder; right, Cigarette Holder. $300.00 – 350.00 set.

Plate 301. Cigarette and match holder combination, 2½"h, 6"l. $175.00 – 200.00.

Plate 303. Chase "Sphere" Cigarette Set: Tray, Cigarette Holder with plastic knob finial, and Lighter, copper. An original set included an open ashtray. $125.00 – 150.00 set.

Plate 302. Cigarette Holder, 2½"h, 3¾"w, porcelain, gold luster finish, made by the Noritake Company, Japan. $100.00 – 120.00.

Plate 304. Figural Porter style Cigarette Set including a Match Holder, Cigarette Holder, and Ashtray in the design, brass, 10"h, unmarked. $160.00 – 175.00.

Plate 305. Cigarette Box, seated nude figure, white metal with a silver finish, holds glass box over her head. The figure is marked "W.B. Mfg. Co." The glass box is the "Ridgeleigh" pattern made by the Heisey Glass Co., Newark, Ohio. $200.00 – 225.00.

Plate 306. "New Yorker" Cigarette Lighter and Cigarette Boxes; chrome combined with rare blue enamel, made by Ronson, Newark, N.J. $300.00 – $400.00.

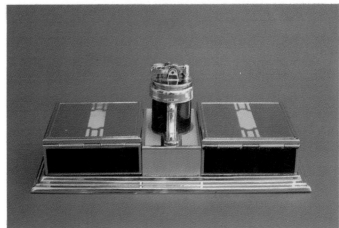

Plate 307. Cigarette Box designed by Walter Von Nessen; brass base covered with a sliding red Bakelite top. $60.00 – 75.00.

Plate 308. Cigarette Box, 5½"l, 5"h, black and red plastic, unmarked. $45.00 – 55.00.

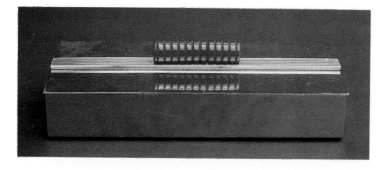

Plate 309. Chase "Band Box," 7⅛"l, cedar lined, divided into three compartments, chrome with red plastic handle. $125.00 – 150.00.

Plate 310. Chase "Bubble" Cigarette Holder, 2½"h, open sphere on square pedestal base, chrome. $45.00 – 55.00.

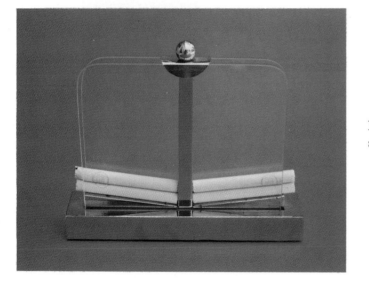

Plate 311. Cigarette and Book Match Holder combination, 9"l, chrome and black plastic, unmarked. $15.00 – 20.00.

Plate 312. Cigarette Holder, chrome and glass, two sections, unmarked. $125.00 – 150.00.

Plate 313. Cigarette Dispenser, nickel plated, studded with red and blue glass stones; Art Metal Works, Newark. N.J., ca. 1928. $150.00 – 200.00.

Plate 314. Cigarette Dispenser, 3"h, silver-plate, French. The top springs open when the small triangular shapes on either side are pressed. $225.00 – 275.00.

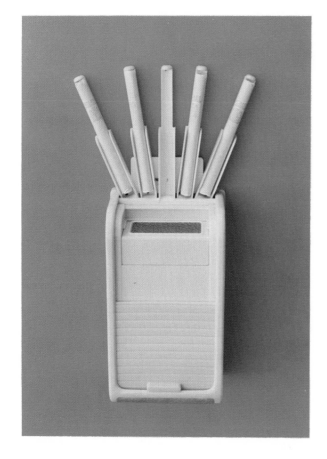

Plate 315. Cigarette Dispenser, 6¼"h, black enamel and chrome. This device opens with a pull spring top. The cigarettes are held by individual metal holders. $200.00 – 225.00.

Plate 316. Cigarette Dispenser, 6"l, plastic. The cigarettes roll out of the case by sliding back the lid, marked "Ziegfield." $75.00 – 85.00.

Plate 318. Cigarette Dispenser, 4¼"h, wedge shaped, burled maple wood. The top of the wedge slides up to reveal the cigarettes. $225.00 – 275.00.

Plate 317. Cigarette Dispenser, 5"h, 7½"l, wood, painted red exterior and black interior. The box has stepped shape when closed. $125.00 – 175.00.

Plate 319. Cigarette Dispenser, 5"h, 3¾"w, book style, wood with green plastic handle. When the lid is raised, music plays. "Musical Cigarettes" printed on side, unmarked. $75.00 – 100.00.

Plate 320. Cigarette Dispenser, 6½"h, cigarette is dispensed from the mouth of a woman wearing a turban; wood with a dark finish; marked "Indel & Graham, San Francisco, 1928." $300.00 – 350.00 (mc).

Plate 321. Evans Cigarette Case and Lighter in original gift box, black enamel and chrome, ca. 1939, American. $175.00 – 225.00.

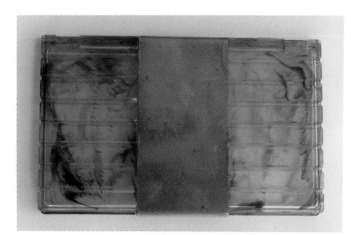

Plate 323. Individual Cigarette Holder, 3"l, dark red plastic studded with amber stones. $50.00 – 60.00.

Plate 322. Cigarette Case, Bakelite and pigskin, sliding top, marked "A. Rolinx, Made in England." $100.00 – 125.00.

Plate 324. Individual Cigarette Holder, 12"l, orange and black plastic. $50.00 – 60.00.

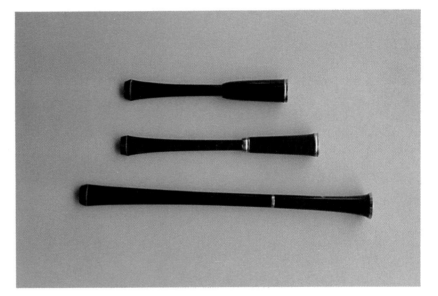

Plate 325. Individual Cigarette Holders, black plastic trimmed with narrow gold bands: top, 2½"l, $20.00 – 30.00; middle, 3"l, $25.00 – 35.00; bottom, 5"l, $30.00 – 40.00.

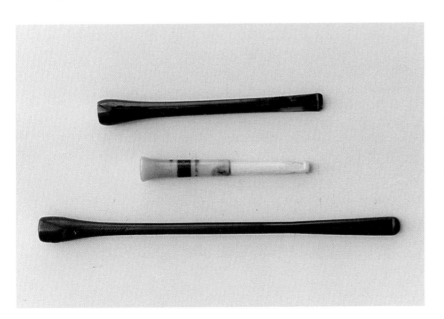

Plate 326. Individual Cigarette Holders: top, 4"l, tortoise shell, $25.00 – 35.00; middle, 3"l, celluloid, $35.00 – 45.00; bottom, 6"l, black plastic, $40.00 – 50.00.

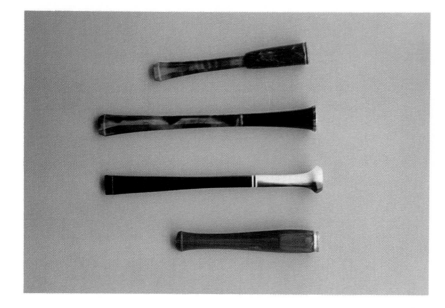

Plate 327. Individual Cigarette Holders: top, blue plastic and tortoise shell, 2½"l; black plastic and tortoise shell, 3½"l; black and white marbled plastic, 3½"l; bottom, blue plastic with silver trim, 2"l. $45.00 – 55.00 each.

Plate 328. Cigar Holder, 4"l, in case with interior of lid marked "Genuine Meerschaum." $140.00 – 160.00.

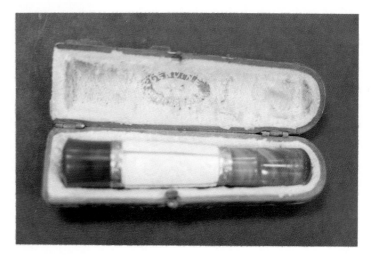

Plate 329. Cigar Clipper, chrome, wooden base, octagonal shape, marked "Alhoso," German. $150.00 – 175.00.

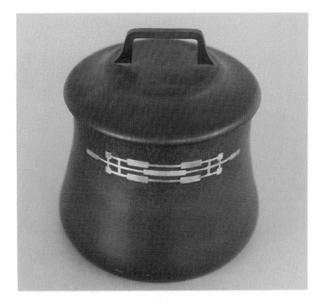

Plate 330. Humidor, 7¼"h, bronze with sterling silver decor, monogrammed and dated "4-4-23," made by the Heintz Art Metal Company. $275.00 – 300.00.

Plate 331. Match Holder, 4"h, attached tray, brass. $70.00 – 80.00.

Plate 332. Pipe Stand, bronze, nude figure poised in diving position, unmarked. $225.00 – 250.00.

Plate 333. Double Pipe Rest, black painted metal base with chrome figure of a golfer swinging a golf club; unmarked, attributed to Art Metal Works, Newark, N. J. $250.00 – 300.00.

Plate 334. Cigarette Strike Lighter, 5"h, figure sits in lotus position, dressed in Oriental robes and headdress; marked "A. M. W., Newark, N. J." (Art Metal Works). $450.00 – 550.00.

Plate 335. Cigarette Strike Lighter in the form of a wine bottle with two chrome wine glasses on either side for cigarettes or matches; solid steel base finished in black enamel, unmarked. $225.00 – 275.00.

Plate 336. Table model Cigarette Lighter, "Bar-Tender" type made by the Art Metal Works of Newark, N. J.; chrome and painted metal, 5½"h, 8"l. $1,800.00 – 2,000.00.

Plate 337. Reverse view of "Bar-Tender" Lighter.

Plate 338. Cigarette Lighter, 4"h x 4"d, electric, ball shape, flanked by a kneeling nude figure with hands held against head; when plugged into an outlet, the wires inside the ball light up; the figure serves as the handle; cast metal painted gold, unmarked. $250.00 – 300.00.

Plate 339. Cigarette Strike Lighter, cast metal with a verdigris finish combined with chrome and marble; a nude figure with arms stretched behind back is in kneeling position to right of lighter; labeled "The Green Goddess Strikalite. Made by Beney Ltd. London, England." "Limousin" is inscribed on base near the flint strip. $350.00 – 400.00.

Plate 340. Cigarette Strike Lighter, ball shape, topped with the figure of a girl standing on one leg with one arm stretched in front of her and one arm stretched behind her; metal with gold finish on marble base; unmarked. $325.00 – 375.00.

Plate 341. Ronson Cigarette Strike Lighter shaped like a sphinx, very rare. $1,000.00 – 1,500.00.

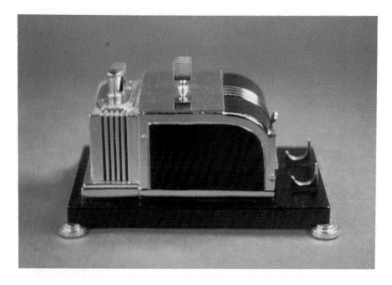

Plate 342. Cigarette Lighter and Dispenser, black enamel and chrome, 4"h, 8"l, made by Ronson. Cigarettes roll out by sliding back the lid on the right side. $350.00 – 400.00.

Plate 343. Thorens table model Cigarette Lighter, wick style; green enamel and gold plated. $125.00 – 175.00.

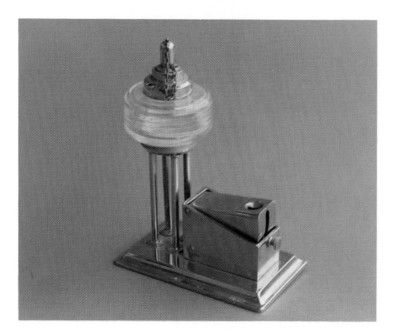

Plate 344. Table model Cigar Lighter with fuel reservoir and clipper; chrome and glass, unmarked. $150.00 – 175.00.

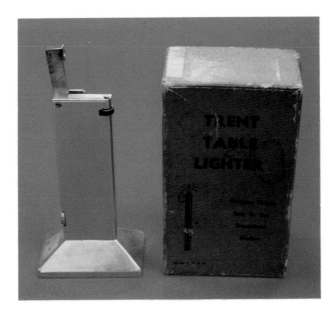

Plate 346. Table model Cigarette Lighter, 4¼"h, chrome; original box marked "Trent Table Lighter. Precision Perfect, Easy To Use, Streamlined, Modern, Made in U. S. A." $75.00 – 100.00.

Plate 345. Table model Cigarette Lighter, 5"h, chrome, three stacked sections form design, unmarked, American. $95.00 – 110.00.

Plate 347. Table model Cigarette Lighter, green and yellow marbled Bakelite, 2"w x 1⅞"h, marked "Evans." $70.00 – 95.00.

Plate 348. Table model Cigarette Lighter, nude figure stands on one leg and holds lighter aloft on raised knee, silver finished metal; marked "Made in U. S. A., W. B. Mfg. Co." $150.00 – 175.00.

Plate 349. Evans table model Cigarette Lighter and Ashtray in original silk lined gift box; a booklet describes the set as "Limoges and Cloisonné"; the tray is signed on the back "H. Gay." $250.00 – 300.00.

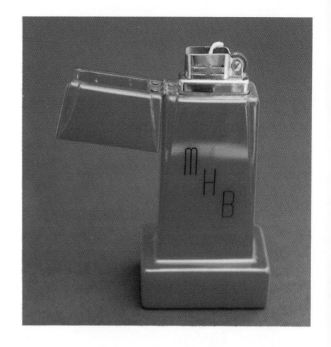

Plate 350. Table model Cigarette Lighter, 6"h x 2¾"w, red Bakelite with initials "MHB" on front, unmarked. $200.00 – 225.00.

Plate 351. Table model Cigarette Lighter and Dispenser, 2½"h x 3"w, shaped like a radio, crocodile finish on body with white composition base; marked "Radio-Lite, Occupied Japan," ca. late 1940s. $70.00 – 85.00.

Plate 352. Table style Cigarette Lighter, 5¾"l, cap and ball pistol design, brass plated with black painted zinc base metal, marked "Made in Japan." $125.00 – 145.00.

Plate 354. Evans Pocket Cigarette Lighter, silver finish accented with a black border and stripe design overlaid with a silver floral pattern. $175.00 – 200.00.

Plate 353. Ronson "Elephant" Cigarette Lighter, table model, chrome with gun-metal base. The piece originally had plastic tusks. $225.00 – 275.00 (mc).

Plate 355. Ronson Pocket Lighter, tortoise shell, chrome trim. $120.00 – 140.00.

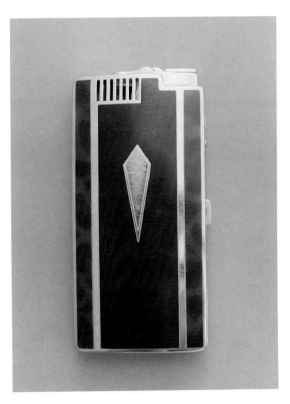

Plate 357. Cigarette Case with Lighter, gun-metal gray finish with silver and black decor; marked "Ronson Lytacase Tuxedo." $150.00 – 200.00.

Plate 356. Pocket Lighters: top, Ronson, tortoise shell, marked with "Pat. Nov. 19-23," $125.00 – 150.00; left, Evans, white enamel with chrome rainbow designs, $100.00 – 125.00; right, Evans, red and black enamel, chrome trim, floral decor combined with stepped designs, $125.00 – 150.00.

Plate 358. Pocket and Purse Lighters: left, gold plated, rocket design on checkerboard background, marked "Royal," $125.00 – 150.00; right, combination lighter and compact, white enamel, gold trim, pink roses, marked "Marathon, Made in U. S. A.," $175.00 – 200.00.

Plate 359. Incense Burner, kneeling nude figure wearing a turban with hands clasped behind her head, metal with dark finish; unmarked, attributed to Art Metal Works, Newark, N. J. $300.00 – 400.00.

Plate 360. Incense Burner, bronze figure, Egyptian influence, Art Metal Works, signed "L. V. Aronson," ca. early 1920s. $400.00 – 500.00.

Plate 361. Incense Burner, figure in Egyptian dress with arms outstretched and one leg bent at knee and the other leg stretched behind her; metal with dark painted finish; marked "L. V. Aronson, c 1924" and "Made in U. S. A." $375.00 – 425.00 (mc).

Plate 362. Incense Burner, cast metal figure, black finish. Egyptian motif, marked "Vantiens, Made in France." $375.00 – 425.00.

131

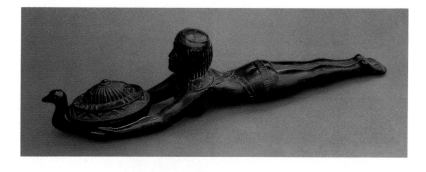

Plate 363. Incense Burner, horizontal semi-nude figure with Egyptian style headdress holding the incense burner which sits on the back of a duck; cast metal with dark black finish; unmarked, attributed to Art Metal Works, Newark, N. J. $300.00 – 400.00

Plate 364. Incense Burner, 13½"l; design is almost identical to burner in preceding photograph except the figure's headdress is longer and there is some variation on the design of the burner; cast metal with a silver finish although color appears gold in photograph, unmarked. $300.00 – 400.00.

Plate 365. Incense Burner, 6½"h, cast iron, floral designs combined with geometric form, marked "Made in France." $150.00 – 175.00.

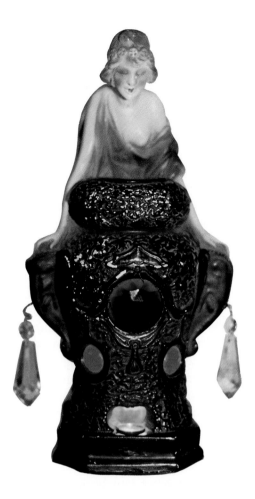

Plate 367. Reverse of Incense Burner in preceding photograph.

Plate 366. Electric Incense Burner, 16"h, 8"w; a semi-draped figure stands behind an ornate stove type structure with a small brass pan in opening for burner; multicolored painted plaster with crystal prisms on each side and three ruby colored glass stones on front. When plugged in, the woman's face is lighted from a bulb in the socket (not visible) which twists upward from the bottom. The ruby stones also glow when lighted. Marked with a paper sticker indicating "Patented March 9, 1925, Design Pat #69,675, S. & S. Mfg. Co., Milwaukee, Wis." $350.00 – 450.00.

Plate 368. Incense Burner, ceramic, 6½"h, figural, Egyptian dress, artist signed, "Lisne," French. $350.00 – 400.00.

133

Statues

Figures, more than any other category of decorative accessory, seem to say "Deco" best. The statues exhibit not only features commonly associated with Art Deco, but also they express the spirit of freedom and optimism in the future that prevailed at the time. It is not surprising that these personifications beguile collectors. As noted earlier, figures were so popular that they were fashioned into dual purpose articles as well as art objects. This section, however, contains only the latter. Statues, statuettes or figurines, and a few head forms or busts are included. (For additional examples of figures, see Ashtrays, Bookends, Candleholders, Incense Burners, and Lamps.)

Most of the Deco figural subjects were women. Pieces were made with couples forming dance partners or duets. Men were also modeled as sportsmen or represented as mythical gods or even circus clowns. Animals made along Deco lines are not so rare as male examples but they are less prevalent than female themes. All kinds of animals, however, were made as decorative sculpture. Members of the cat family (jaguar, panther, tiger) and deer, elk, and gazelles as well as dogs (like the greyhound) projected the essential components of the Deco image — speed, grace, and sleekness. Certain animals, especially dogs, were often part of female dominated scenes. Even birds such as cockatoos, ducks, parrots, and penguins were shaped in stylized forms to fit in with modern decor.

The nude or semi-nude female apparently was the favorite figural topic of the period. It is held in no less esteem by collectors. Poses varied from languid, reclining positions to ones expressing movement. Grace and speed were implied by various dance positions or hair shaped as wings or fashioned in a "wind blown" style. Kneeling or standing figures with arms stretched forward symbolized movement into the future. Arms stretched overhead, perhaps holding a globe or sphere, seem to indicate awareness and interest in the world at large.

While the nude and semi-nude figures may suggest the spirit of the period, fully clothed models portray the dress and hair styles in vogue. Interest in other cultures was also exhibited by the figure's costume. The Egyptian influence was dominant in the mid 1920s, after the opening of King Tut's tomb in 1923. Several of the figures shown in this section and some in other categories (see Lamps and Incense Burners) flaunt the trappings of Egyptian attire such as metal breastplates, harem pants, and elaborate headdresses. Female figures with black finishes show the influence of African art and black American entertainers. Jazz musicians and torch singers became very popular during the 1920s, especially in France.

Decorative figures not only were made in a number of sizes and poses, but also they were made from many different materials, including bronze, copper, metal alloys, plaster, pottery, and porcelain. The French bronzes are the most coveted and most expensive. Bronze combined with ivory and precious jewels, silver or gold is called "chryselephantine" work. D.H. Chiparus, who worked in France, is noted to have excelled in this type of sculpture. Prices for his original pieces are in the the tens of thousands of dollars today. Collectors should be aware, however, that current bronze manufacturers reproduce or imitate some of his figures as well as several other famous sculptors of the period.

Because bronzes were expensive to manufacture, it did not take entrepreneurs long to recognize the value of mass producing similar statues from metal alloys. Pot metal, white metal, or spelter are names frequently used to identify such alloys. Pseudo bronze figures were made in both Europe and America. Even if a piece can be identified as being of French origin, do not assume the metal is bronze. Many of the pot metal pieces were executed quite well. Different patinations and finishes were used to give either a bronze look or colored surface. Some were even made with ivory faces and hands, imitating chryselephantine types. Fabricated ivory, often called "ivorene," was sometimes used, however.

Patination and cold painted are two terms used to describe bronze finishes. Patination refers to a colored finish which is fired onto the metal and thus becomes permanent. Cold painted means the finish was not fired onto the metal. Lacquer was applied to preserve the color, but this type of finish is not totally permanent. Some of the metal alloy figures were simply painted without any sealing coat. Consequently, over time, the paint has chipped or become noticeably worn. Those with apparent surface damage can sometimes be purchased for bargain prices. Dealers have them repainted, but prices should not be the same as for those in good or original condition. Inspect figures carefully for detail to note signs of age and wear on finishes as well as whether there are chips on the face, hair, or limbs.

Because of the demand for deco figures, pot metal statues are far from cheap. Those in good condition, depending on size, will cost several hundred dollars. It is not uncommon for examples to cost $1000 or more, especially if it can be determined the piece was made in France. It is rare to find any authentic deco metal figure for less than $100.

Porcelain figures were made by several European factories during the Art Deco era. The Royal Dux Company of Czechoslovakia created a number of designs. Some examples are included here. Some firms who were more famous for producing table wares also made figural items during that time. The German Hutschenreuther Company is just one example. American porcelain is quite scarce compared to European. But the Lenox china company in Trenton, New Jersey, made porcelain figures which portrayed Deco themes. See one example in the Lamps section. Porcelain figures are usually less expensive than metal statues. Price is often related to size and the larger the porcelain figure, the more costly.

Earthenware or simple pottery figures were also made in this country and abroad. Usually earthenware items are less expensive than those made of hard paste porcelain or bone china. Not only was the manufacturing process cheaper, but also earthenware is not as strong. It chips and breaks easily and also can become discolored or crazed over time. Pottery figures, however, are often comparable or higher in price than porcelain ones. Those made by American art potteries are very collectible. Some American companies, which produced inexpensive pottery dishes and accessories, also made a few figures. Such items were not the company's main product, and thus the figures are scarce, as well as popular, and bring high prices compared with other items they manufactured.

The statues and figurines are grouped here according to their composition. Ceramic (porcelain and pottery), Plaster, and Metals (brass, bronze, chrome, copper, and metal alloys).

Plate 369. Left: Porcelain Figure, 7¼"h, elegantly clad woman wearing a long, tailored dress with coat; a hat, purse, and high heels complete the outfit; a small dog stands by her feet; highly glazed white porcelain; "KNEIL-WEIN" impressed on base; ca. 1930s, European. Right: Figure similar to the one on the left except the woman is not wearing a coat as part of her ensemble, and she is bending over with her left arm touching the dog's face as he stands with his front legs resting on her knees; the base is also a different design, and it is inscribed only with "KNEIL." $1,000.00 – 1,200.00 each.

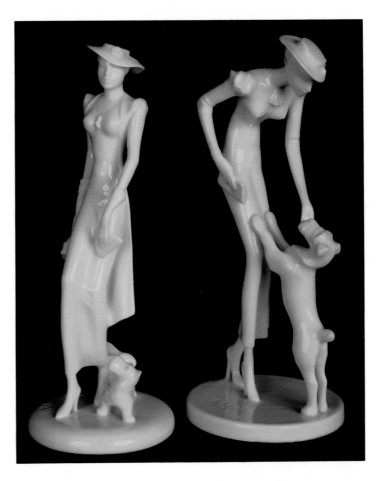

Plate 370. Royal Dux Porcelain Figure, 21"h, barefoot girl, posed in a dancing position; dressed in a cobalt blue midriff top and long white skirt decorated with blue flowers, Czechoslovakian. $1,200.00 – 1,400.00.

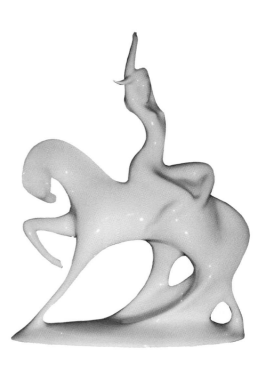

Plate 371. Royal Dux Porcelain Figure, 13"h, nude girl with arms stretched overhead sits in a reverse position on top of a prancing horse; undecorated white porcelain. $350.00 – 400.00.

Plate 372. Royal Dux Porcelain Figure, 8"h, nude woman sitting on one leg with the other leg raised at an angle and arms stretched forward holding a bottle. $250.00 – 300.00.

Plate 373. Royal Dux Porcelain Figure of a clown playing an accordion, 12"h. $500.00 – 600.00.

Plate 374. Figure of a dancer with fan, 12"h, porcelain, mounted on metal base, attributed to Herwig & Co., Germany, ca. 1930s. $275.00 – 325.00.

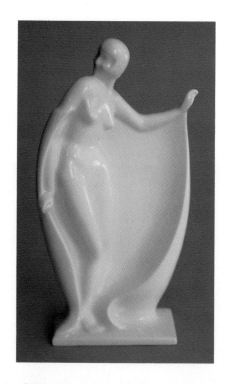

Plate 375. Dancing Figure holding end of long, full skirt above her head, porcelain, Herwig & Co., Germany, ca. 1930s. $300.00 – 350.00.

Plate 376. Limoges Figure, 9"h, nude holding drape or perhaps a large towel outstretched behind her body, undecorated white porcelain. $275.00 – 325.00.

Plate 377. Vanity Bust of a woman wearing a large hat and looking over her shoulder; Royal Dux Porcelain, artist signed "Elly Strobach." $325.00 – 375.00.

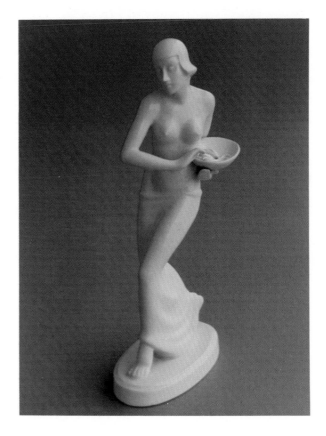

Plate 379. Semi-nude Figure, 11"h, ceramic, Egyptian influence, marked "Kent Art Ware," Japanese. $150.00 – 175.00.

Plate 378. Ceramic Figure modeled after Dorothy Lamour, film star famous for wearing a sarong. The statuette was made by the Clark Pottery of East Palestine, Ohio, ca. 1940s. $175.00 – 200.00.

Plate 380. Frankoma Pottery Figure, 5¾"h, "Weeping Lady," Desert Gold color, ca. late 1930s, American. $175.00 – 225.00.

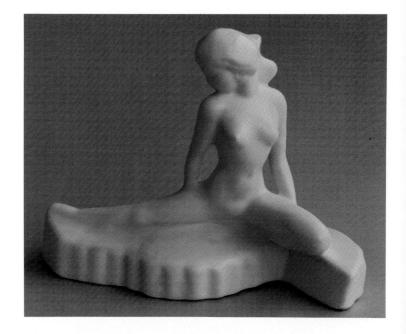

Plate 381. Vanity Doll Head, 5½"h, ceramic, marked "G & K Keramik, Made in Austria." $160.00 – 180.00.

Plate 382. Nude Figure posed in dance position, ceramic, 8½"h, 11"l, made by the Camden Art and Tile Co., Camden, Arkansas. $150.00 – 175.00.

Plate 383. Figure, kneeling nude shedding drape, 10"h, porcelain, white matte finish, octagonal shaped base; German, signed "Poerzl," with G. Greiner factory mark, ca. late 1920s. The artist was a noted German designer of metals and ceramics. $800.00 – 900.00.

Plate 384. Royal Dux Porcelain Hound, 11"l, dark brown glaze on white base. $175.00 – 225.00.

Plate 385. Frankoma Pottery Puma Figures, dark black glaze; left, standing puma, 7½ h; right, reclining puma, 9½"l, ca. mid 1930s, originally; produced through the early 1960s and again from 1972 to 1983. $200.00 – 250.00 each for original version.

Plate 386. Tigers, porcelain, 9½"l, overall, German, made by the Hutschenreuther Company, ca. early 1920s. $700.00 – 800.00.

Plate 387. Pair of ceramic birds, high glaze green finish, signed "Ch. Lemanceau," French designer of pottery animals. $300.00 – 350.00.

Plate 388. Figure of a stag with head raised upward, ceramic, pink glaze, marked "Pacific, made in U.S.A." $15.00 – 25.00.

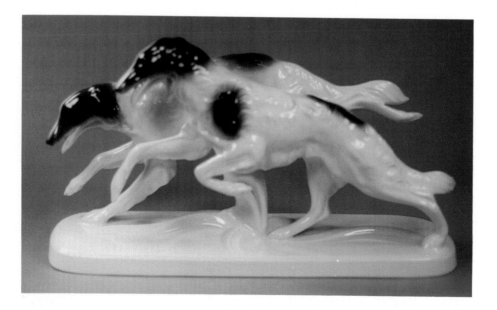

Plate 389. Pair of Russian wolfhounds, 13"l overall, ceramic, German, signed "B. Kopecki," ca. 1940s. $250.00 – 300.00.

Plate 391. Reclining woman in long gown posed with greyhound, 25"l overall, plaster, marked "Pecchioli." $275.00 – 325.00.

Plate 390. Mannekin Head, 10"h, plaster, gold finish. $175.00 – 200.00.

Plate 392. Woman modeled with wolfhounds, 14"l, 12"h, faux marble, marked "A Santini." $450.00 – 500.00. (A similar version has been reproduced.)

Plate 393. Semi-nude Figure posed in dance position, 21"h overall, white metal, bronze finish, mounted on black marble base; marked "Fayral," French, ca. 1920s. $2,000.00 – 2,200.00.

143

Plate 394. Bronze Sculpture, "Diana," on marble base, 18½"l; "Diana" (the Huntress), 9"h, posed with a bow; hunting dogs, 8"h, posed in a leaping position, French, $1,000.00 – 1,200.00.

Plate 395. Semi-nude Figure and canine posed in reclining position; pot metal, black matte finish, gold accents, mounted on a marble base, 16½"l overall, marked "France." $1,400.00 – 1,600.00.

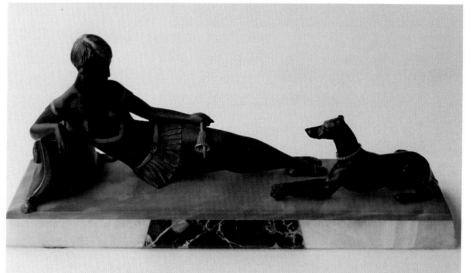

Plate 396. Pair of wolfhounds, 30"l overall, bronze, mounted on a marble base, French. $900.00 – 1,000.00.

Plate 398. Pair of penguins, 4¼"h, brass, unmarked. $250.00 – 300.00 pair.

Plate 397. Copper Figure, 14"h, bronze finish, Egyptian influence. $600.00 – 700.00.

Plate 399. Figure of a woman, 10"h, Spanish style dress; pot metal and ivorene mounted on a marble base. $275.00 – 325.00.

Plate 400. Bronze Figure, 6"h, girl with bare midriff has arms outstretched and holds an end of her skirt in each hand, mounted on round marble base, ca. 1920s. $225.00 – 275.00.

Plate 401. Bronze Figure dressed in an elaborate harem style costume and headdress; mounted on a black marble base; unmarked, European. $1,200.00 – 1,400.00.

Plate 402. Chrome Figure, 4½"h, girl holding fan-shaped skirt, square marble base, unmarked, American. $120.00 – 145.00.

Plate 403. Chiparus-type Figure, 7"h, pot metal, red lacquered finish, ivory face, marble base. (A similar figure has been reproduced.) $350.00 – 450.00.

Plate 404. Bronze Figure, 9¾"h, nude girl with one hand on hip and the other holding a large open container, unmarked. $275.00 – 325.00.

Plate 405. Bronze Figure of a swimmer posed in diving position, 5½"h, marble base, unmarked, American. $175.00 – 225.00.

Plate 406. Chrome Figure, 4"h, nude girl with drape around shoulders sits with arms clasped around bent knees; onyx base, ca. 1920s. $125.00 – 175.00.

Plate 407. Chrome-plated Figure in an abstract stylized form standing on one leg with the other raised and bent at knee; one arm extended in front of face and one behind back; unmarked, attributed to Art Metal Works, Newark, N. J. $800.00 – 1,000.00.

Plate 408. Chrome Figure, 5"l, nude girl sitting with one leg bent at knee and the other stretched behind her with arms raised. This piece was originally a hood ornament for a car, called a "car mascot." $275.00 – 325.00.

Table Wares

Companies engaged in manufacturing products for preparing and serving food found it necessary to accommodate the new trends in modern design. Streamlined and angular shapes can be found not only in sets of china but in kitchen equipment as well. In this section, table wares are not confined to dishes but include other utilitarian and decorative pieces. Because of the great diversity of this category, it is possible to show only a sample of items, but the pieces illustrated should alert collectors to the many possibilities table wares offer.

Angular shapes or stylized designs cut or molded into glass table wares were made to grace the dining tables of the period. Art glass by French manufacturers is usually too expensive for moderate collectors. But, many types of inexpensive table glass were made during the 1930s and 1940s by American factories. Depression era glass collectors began to salvage pieces during the 1960s. A number of the patterns have unmistakable Deco characteristics. "Manhattan," a clear glass pattern made by Anchor Hocking is just one type finding its way into Deco collections. The ruby red, cobalt blue, and deep green colored glass made by other American glass companies also qualifies as Deco. Quite a few pieces are very attractive, some are even elegant and others are just amusing.

Flatware, serving pieces, and decorative table articles can be found in silver, brass, copper, chrome, and plated metals. Chrome and plated metals are the least expensive. Nude or semi-nude figures were made into metal centerpieces or candleholders. Prices are competitive with other figural items and examples are just as much in demand. A number of metal Deco items were originally silver plated. Because the plating wears off, items become ugly and lose much of their value. Dealers have found it lucrative to have such objects stripped to the base metal which was usually copper or brass. The copper centerpiece with a pot metal nude is an example which was once silver plated. Do not automatically disregard badly worn plated pieces which have obvious Deco signs. It may be wise to have them stripped and polished by a commercial firm which specializes in that kind of work.

Ceramics include earthenware or semi-china, stoneware, and porcelain. Simplified decoration distinguished Deco china from that produced during the Victorian years. Floral transfer patterns covering the entire surface of china gave way to colored line borders or abstract geometric patterns.

Sometimes china was left undecorated with the shape or mold drawing attention to a modern image. Geometric shapes other than the usual circular form are seen here in the rectangular bowl and the triangular shaped cup and saucer.

Ceramic table wares can be found at all price levels. Pieces designed and hand painted by Clarice Cliff for the Royal Staffordshire Pottery during the late 1920s and early 1930s are highly regarded by advanced collectors. Price can reach several hundred to several thousand dollars for some examples, especially those with floral and landscape decor. "Bizarre," "Geometric," and "Fantasque" were some of the pattern names. The English artist's signature was included in most of her work. Pieces which do not have her name or signature as part of the mark are usually considerably lower in price.

The "Biarritz" soup bowl shown here is one such example. Although the pattern is quite simple, it also merits consideration as a form of Deco table ware. Deco patterns by other English potters are also quite collectible. Many good examples in the moderate price ranges are surfacing. These may be found mixed in with other miscellaneous dishes by dealers who do not specialize in Art Deco.

"American Modern," designed by Russel Wright for the Ohio-based Steubenville Pottery is also quite collectible and much lower in price. This line was made from about 1939 through the late 1950s. Solid colored surfaces without other added decoration implied a modern concept. Many other European and American pottery and porcelain factories produced their own renditions of modern style. Japanese table ware companies used similar interpretations to reach the large American market. Deco patterned china made by the Noritake firm has been attracting many collectors during the last few years. Prices are still affordable but not inconsequential. Table china however, is probably the largest source of Art Deco "sleepers" and possible bargains today.

The Table Wares shown here are grouped by the above three categories: glass, metal, and ceramics (porcelain and pottery).

Plate 409. Candleholders, 6½"h, clear glass with etched pattern on base and flared "sunburst" molded design around top, made by the New Martinsville Glass Company, New Martinsville, Virginia, ca. 1920s. $70.00 – 90.00 pair.

Plate 410. New Martinsville "Radiance" Candleholders in dark ruby red glass. $100.00 – 120.00 pair.

Plate 411. Cambridge "Rubena" glass Candleholders, 8½"h. $250.00 – 275.00.

Plate 412. Cambridge "Calla Lily" Candleholders, 6½"h, topaz colored glass. $80.00 – 100.00 pair.

Plate 413. Cambridge Candleholders, 8"h, sapphire blue glass. $90.00 – 110.00 pair.

Plate 414. Candleholder, 8½"h, amber glass, a series of hexagon shapes compose column, terminating in a similarly shaped base, unmarked. $150.00 – 175.00.

Plate 416. Candleholders, 7"h, amethyst glass with faceted stems, unmarked. $120.00 – 145.00 pair.

Plate 415. Candleholder, 7"h, clear glass, sharp angular shape, unmarked. $25.00 – 30.00.

Plate 418. Centerpiece, Floral Frog, 7"h, 7"d, designed as a ship on water in frosted blue glass similar to Candleholders in preceding photograph, English origin. $90.00 – 110.00.

Plate 417. Candleholders, 5½"h, frosted blue glass, sailboat theme. $65.00 – 75.00 pair.

Plate 419. Centerpiece, 4"h, 7¼"d, light green glass, diamond shape, molded fan designs on body, pierced at top to hold flowers, unmarked. $75.00 – 95.00.

Plate 421. Centerpiece, Floral Frog, 6½"h, Cambridge Glass, clear, figure of a nude in a different "Bashful Charlotte" design. $100.00 – 125.00.

Plate 420. Centerpiece, Floral Frog, 9"h, Cambridge glass, clear, figure of a nude with hands over her face ("Bashful Charlotte"), 6½" h. $85.00 – 110.00.

Plate 422. Centerpiece, Floral Frog, Cambridge glass, clear, figure of a seagull in flight, 11½"h. $60.00 – 75.00.

Plate 423. Centerpiece Bowl, 9"h, free-form shape in light blue glass with frosted panels on front and back, stepped base, unmarked. $200.00 – 225.00.

Plate 424. Centerpiece Bowl, pink frosted glass, triangular shape with stepped base; hand-painted black nude figure on each side. (Originally, the bowl had a pair of matching Candleholders.) $175.00 – 200.00.

Plate 425. Centerpiece, Compote, 6"h, 5¼"d; Cambridge "Crown Tuscan" glass; nude figure supports bowl, pink opaque glass. $150.00 – 175.00.

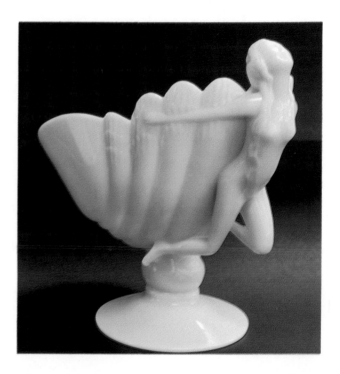

Plate 426. Centerpiece, Shell Bowl on short pedestal base; Cambridge "Crown Tuscan" glass; nude figure with long hair has legs bent and arms stretched behind back decorating exterior of bowl, 10½"h x 12"w. $275.00 – 300.00.

Plate 427. Divided Dish, light green glass inserted on top of a chrome triangular shaped holder with figural nudes ("Bashful Charlottes") at each corner, Cambridge. $300.00 – 350.00.

Plate 428. Covered Dish, triangular shaped clear glass in chrome holder decorated with "Bashful Charlottes" at each corner, unmarked, attributed to the Cambridge Glass Company. $225.00 – 275.00.

Plate 429. "Square" design by Cambridge in clear glass; Bowl, 8¼"d, divided into three sections on a square base. $35.00 – 40.00.

Plate 430. Compote, 2¾"h x 6"d, "Queen Mary" pattern Depression glass; clear, vertical ribbed design; made by the Anchor Hocking Glass Company of Ohio, ca. late 1930s. $10.00 – 12.00. Matching Sherbet Dishes, 2"h x 3¾"d. $6.00 – 8.00 each.

Plate 431. Serving Bowl, "Manhattan" pattern in clear glass, made by Anchor Hocking, ca. late 1930s. $20.00 – 25.00.

Plate 432. Covered Candy Jar, clear glass, "Manhattan" pattern. $30.00 – 35.00.

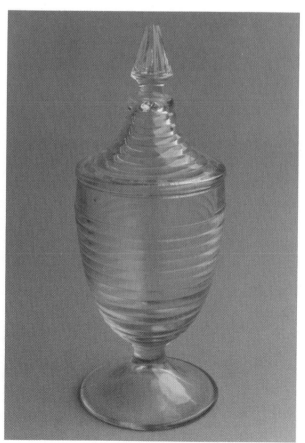

Plate 433. Serving Bowl, 12"d, "Windsor Diamond" pattern in pink glass, made by the Jeanette Glass Company, ca. 1930s. $25.00 – 35.00.

Plate 434. Pitcher, 7"h, "Windsor Diamond" pattern in clear glass. $30.00 – 40.00. Matching glasses with pedestal bases. Left, $18.00 – 20.00; right, 12.00 – 14.00.

Plate 435. Pitcher, 8½"h, and Tumblers, 4½"h (set of four), vertical and horizontal ribbed pattern, pink glass, made by Jeanette Glass. $85.00 – 100.00.

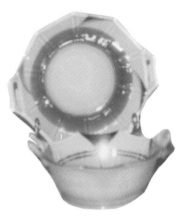

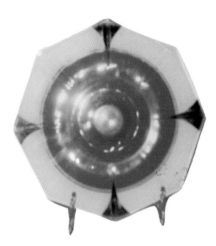

Plate 436. Bowls, Czechoslovakian glass, angular shapes decorated with a bright orange inner border (top) and a brilliant yellow and black decor (bottom), ca. 1920s. $70.00 – 85.00 each.

Plate 437. Cake Stand, short pedestal base, Czechoslovakian glass; vivid red color decorates center of dish with an opaque white border accented with black designs. $80.00 – 100.00.

Plate 438. Bowl, white opaque glass with clear glass center; the widely scalloped border is divided into four red "V" shaped sections, outlined in black, Czechoslovakian. $65.00 – 80.00.

Plate 439. Plate, 8¼"d, "Dancing Nymphs" pattern in clear glass, made by the Consolidated Glass Company of Pennsylvania, ca. 1928. $200.00 – 250.00.

Plate 440. Creamer and Sugar, 3½"h, Cambridge glass "Square" design in light amber glass on black base. $40.00 – 50.00 pair.

Plate 441. Creamer and Sugar Set on handled Tray in light green glass with ribbed pattern, Cambridge. $80.00 – 100.00.

Plate 442. Creamer and Sugar Set, 3"h, pink glass, sharp angular handles, made by the Tiffin Glass Company, Tiffin, Ohio. $30.00 – 35.00 pair.

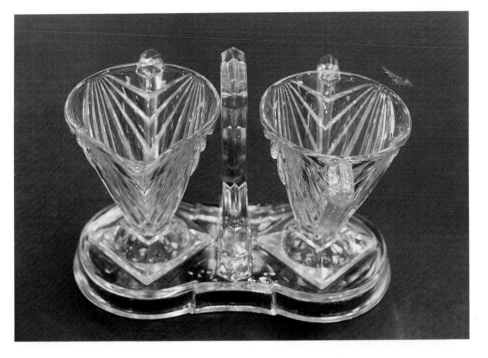

Plate 443. Creamer and Sugar Set on handled Tray, "Pyramid" pattern in light amber glass, made by the Indiana Glass Company, ca. late 1920s. $100.00 – 125.00.

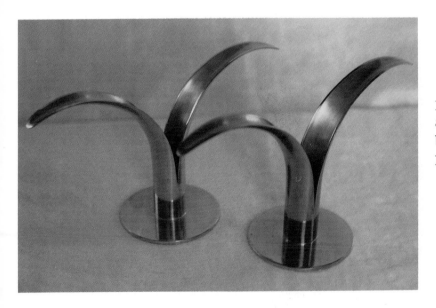

Plate 444. Brass Candleholders, 4¾"h x 8¾"w, split leaf design on round base; made by Ystad-Metall, Sweden. $80.00 – 95.00 pair.

Plate 445. Chrome "Porpoise" Candleholders, 4"d, 1"h, chamberstick style with a black porpoise serving as a handle, made by the Chase Company. $75.00 – 90.00 pair.

Plate 446. Chrome Candleholder, 10½"h, fashioned with the stem designed as a nude dancing figure on Bakelite and chrome base, unmarked. $125.00 – 150.00.

Plate 447. Chrome Candleholders, 2½"h, and Flower Bowl, 3½"h, deep midnight blue mirror base; "Bubble" design by Chase. $160.00 – 175.00 set.

Plate 448. Copper Candleholders, 2½"h, with white plastic square base; "Bubble" design by Chase. $40.00 – 55.00 pair.

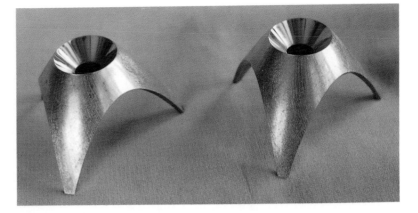

Plate 449. Nickel silver Candleholders, 1¾"h x 3¾"w, triangular shape, marked "AS-Soligen, Germany (des. patent pending)." $70.00 – 85.00 pair.

Plate 450. Candleholders, 5"h, sterling on bronze, made by the Heintz Art Metal Company, Buffalo, New York. $300.00 – 350.00 pair.

Plate 451. Stainless steel Candleholders, three light style individually mounted on a raised step of the rectangular base, unmarked, attributed to European origin. $80.00 – 100.00 pair.

Plate 452. Candleholder, 15"h, two light, pot metal figure, silver finish, mounted on a mahogany stand, English. $375.00 – 425.00.

Plate 453. Chrome and glass Compote, 9"h x 8½"d; nude girl with long hair holds bowl, unmarked. $125.00 – 150.00.

Plate 454. Compote, 9½"h, brass, abstract figures posed in dance position support bowl, ca. 1930s, unmarked. $300.00 – 350.00.

Plate 455. Compote, 6"h, 7"d, chrome by Farberware; nude figure supports open-work designed bowl, American. $80.00 – 100.00.

Plate 456. Centerpiece: Console Bowl, 8½" x 3¼", matching Candleholders, chrome, unmarked. $125.00 – 150.00 set.

Plate 457. Centerpiece: Compote with Candleholders attached to Tray, marked "Farberware, Brooklyn, N. Y." $200.00 – 225.00.

Plate 458. Centerpiece: Flower Bowl, 10"d, and matching Candleholders, 1⅞"h x 3½"d, "Diana" design by Chase; copper and white plastic. $80.00 – 95.00 set.

Plate 459. Centerpiece Dish, 10"d, footed base; brass, silver, and copper fashioned into an abstract geometric design, artist signed, made in Mexico. $125.00 – 150.00.

Plate 460. Centerpiece, 12"d, copper bowl with a pot metal nude figure holding a bird bath designed as a frog, originally silver plated, unmarked. $300.00 – 350.00.

Plate 461. Centerpiece, 9"h, white metal with an enameled green finish; nude figure supports bowl, made by the Frankart Company, New York City, ca. 1920s. $500.00 – 600.00.

Plate 462. Brass Coffee Service. The set includes a Coffee Pot with warmer, Creamer, Sugar, and Tray, ca. 1930s, marked "Doryln Silversmith." $350.00 – 400.00.

Plate 463. Chrome Coffee Service: Urn, 12"h, Creamer and Sugar, 4"h, Tray, 18¾ l; smooth polished surface with black Bakelite handles and finials, made by the Manning-Bowman Company, Meriden, Connecticut. $250.00 – 300.00.

Plate 464. Chrome Coffee Service: Urn, 15½"h, Covered Sugar and Covered Creamer, 6"h, one handle design; oval Tray, 17"l; etched pattern on polished chrome with rare green marbled Bakelite handles and finials; made by the Manning-Bowman Company. $600.00 – 700.00 set.

Plate 466. Chrome and white ceramic Tea Set: Teapot, 7½"h; one handled open Sugar, 2"h x 4½"w; one handled Creamer, 2"h x 5½"w; English. $125.00 – 145.00 set.

Plate 465. Chrome Coffee Urn, 15½"h x 12"w, Bakelite trim, sphere shape with large bail style handle; manufactured by Manning-Bowman. $250.00 – 275.00 set.

Plate 467. Chrome Percolator, 12"h, round body on pedestal base, marked "Keystoneware." $120.00 – 140.00.

Plate 468. Chrome Creamer and Sugar sit back to back on round Tray, black Bakelite handles, made by the Manning-Bowman Company. $70.00 – 80.00 set.

Plate 470. Silver-plated Egg Cups with square Tray accented with a Bakelite knob on handle, unmarked. $65.00 – 80.00.

Plate 469. Copper Coffee Pot, 13"h, wooden handle and finial, American. $140.00 – 150.00.

Plate 471. Brass and plastic Napkin Holder, 6¹⁄₁₆"l x 4⅛"w, fitted with a ball-shaped weight to keep napkins in place, Chase. $40.00 – 50.00 set.

Plate 472. Chrome and plastic Serving Fork and Spoon, 10⅛"l, Chase. $45.00 – 55.00 set.

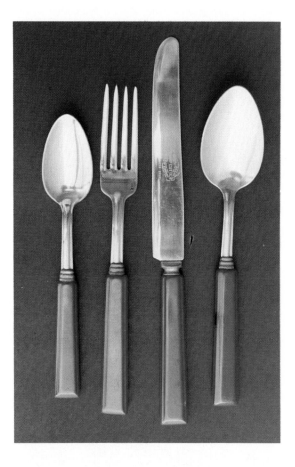

Plate 474. Electric Toaster, chrome with black trim, made by Sunbeam Electric Company, American. $75.00 – 100.00.

Plate 473. Flatware Place Setting, stainless steel with red Bakelite handles. $30.00 – 35.00 set.

Plate 475. Chrome Crumber Set, black plastic trim, unmarked. $30.00 – 40.00.

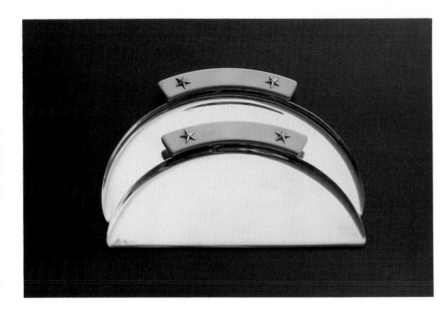

Plate 476. Chrome "Tidy" Crumber set by Chase; crescent moon shape with white plastic handles. $50.00 – 65.00 set.

Plate 477. Plastic Crumb Tray with red Bakelite handle pierced to hang, carmel color, unmarked. $50.00 – 60.00.

Plate 478. Porcelain Berry Set, angular flared scalloped mold; white body design highlighted with red outlining; Reinhold Schlegelmilch Company, Tillowitz, Silesia (R.S. Tillowitz), ca. 1930s. $160.00 – 180.00 set.

Plate 479. Serving Dish, porcelain, square shape with open handles; abstract design in gold around outer border and in center with a multicolored banner around inner border; R. S. Tillowitz (Royal Silesia mark). $30.00 – 40.00.

Plate 480. Dessert Bowl, porcelain, hexagon shape decorated with multicolored birds and stylized flowers; R. S. Tillowitz. $15.00 – 20.00.

Plate 481. Creamer and Covered Syrup Pitcher, porcelain; hand-painted stylized leaf decor in fall colors on a tan background; R. S. Tillowitz. Creamer, $15.00 – 20.00; syrup, $40.00 – 50.00.

Plate 482. Serving Pieces decorated with the same pattern as the preceding pieces: Bread Tray, $120.00 – 140.00; Square Dish with open handles, $35.00 – 45.00; Leaf-shaped Bowl with Under-plate, $45.00 – 55.00.

Plate 483. Bavarian and Limoges porcelain blanks hand-painted with a colorful abstract design by the Juh. H. Brauer Studio of Chicago. Cake Plate, $100.00 – 125.00; Creamer and Sugar, $100.00 – 120.00 set.

Plate 484. Compote, 3½"h, 9¼"d, porcelain, hand-painted silver butterflies on dark green background, artist signed; French Limoges porcelain, American decoration. $80.00 – 100.00.

Plate 485. Compote, 3"h, 6½"d, porcelain, bold orange, black, and white abstract designs on gold lustre background; made by the Noritake Company, Japan. $80.00 – 100.00.

Plate 486. Japanese porcelain decorated with orange and yellow flowers on a blue background with a lustre finish. Cereal or Soup Bowl, $20.00 – 25.00; Cracker Jar, $40.00 – 50.00.

Plate 487. Serving Bowl, 10½"l, black and multicolored leaves on orange background, lustre finish, gold trim, Japanese porcelain. $30.00 – 40.00.

Plate 489. Demitasse Cup and Saucer, porcelain, black and gray diamond pattern on white background; Hutschenreuther Porcelain Company, Germany. $30.00 – 40.00.

Plate 488. Covered Sugar Bowl, 5¼"h, orange and yellow zig-zag design, lustre finish Japanese porcelain. $35.00 – 40.00.

Plate 490. Coffee Cup and Saucer, English, Royal Doulton china; "Carnival" pattern in orange, black, yellow, and blue on white background, ca. 1930s. $40.00 – 50.00.

Plate 491. Coffee Cup and Saucer, porcelain, hand-painted cobalt blue tapered bands divide pieces into four sections decorated with gold flowers with a cobalt blue center; Mäbendorf porcelain, ca. 1920s, German. $60.00 – 75.00.

Plate 492. Coffee Cup and Saucer, porcelain, hand-painted black on white abstract border extending on each corner through wide yellow inner border on saucer; cup decorated with cameos of a silhouette of a Cupid and bird on white against yellow background; the same black and white decor as on saucer divides the cup into four sections; Mäbendorf porcelain. $70.00 – 85.00.

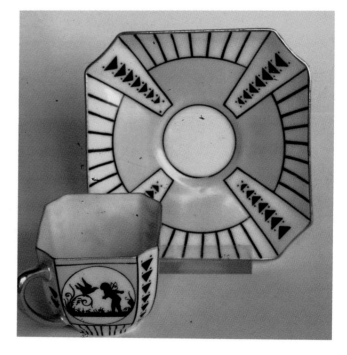

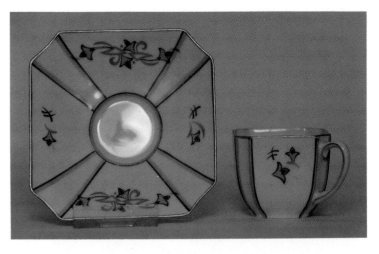

Plate 494. Coffee Cup and Saucer, Mäbendorf porcelain, red and blue stylized floral design, gold trim. $55.00 – 70.00.

Plate 493. Coffee Cup and Saucer, porcelain, same shape as preceding cups, decorated with a very dark green glaze accented with gold tapered bands overlaid with a dark green triangle and dot pattern dividing pieces into four sections; Mäbendorf porcelain. $75.00 – 90.00.

Plate 495. Chocolate Set: Pot, 8½"h; Cup, 2½"h, and Saucer; Creamer and Sugar, 3½"h, porcelain decorated with hand-painted multicolored birds and flowers on a light brown background with wide dark brown borders, gold handles and finials; bird decor is only on the chocolate pot; marked "Made in Japan." $300.00 – 350.00 set for four.

Plate 496. Pitcher, 3¼"h, porcelain, hand-painted cobalt blue flower surrounded by large yellow-orange and green colored spheres with narrow red trim on handle and neck, Czechoslovakian. $30.00 – 35.00.

Plate 497. Pitcher, 3½"h, porcelain, wide pink bands outlined in black alternate with narrow double black bands on white, Czechoslovakian. $50.00 – 55.00.

Plate 498. Pitcher, 7"h, porcelain, Penguin figure, made by the Theodore Haviland Company, Limoges, France; signed by Edouard Sandoz, French artist noted for his Art Deco animal figures in porcelain and bronze, ca. 1920s. Other table figures designed by Sandoz for Haviland included ducks, fish, and monkeys. $375.00 – 425.00.

Plate 499. Candleholder, 4"h, "Tuscany" pattern made by the Roseville Pottery, Roseville, Ohio, ca. 1927. $35.00 – 45.00.

Plate 500. Centerpiece Bowl, 11"l, with Floral Frog, "Tuscany" pattern by Roseville. $100.00 – 125.00.

Plate 501. Centerpiece Bowl, 3"h, 11"d, ceramic; black and green swag and tassel decor with woman's cameo outlined in black; triangular pierced work on border, unmarked, attributed to the Weller Pottery, Zanesville, Ohio. $65.00 – 75.00.

Plate 502. Centerpiece Bowl, 6"h, 11"d, ceramic; diamond shape, stepped sides and base; orange, black, and green hand-painted work on white body; Myott and Son Pottery Company, England. $80.00 – 100.00.

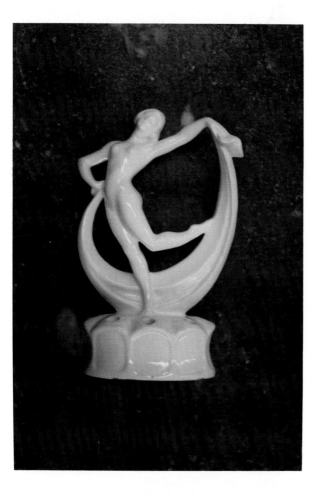

Plate 503. Centerpiece Floral Frog, 7"h, ceramic, dancing nude figure, glossy white glaze, marked "Germany." $70.00 – 85.00.

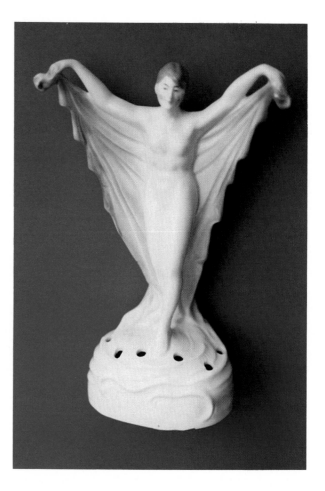

Plate 504. Centerpiece Floral Frog, 13½"h, nude figure holding full length veil; white finish except for hand-painted hair and facial features; marked "Coronet" (an American importer) and "Made in Germany." $120.00 – 140.00.

Plate 505. Demitasse Cup and Saucer, ceramic, triangular shape, "Tricorn" design in orange and white, made by the Salem China Company, Salem, Ohio. $20.00 – 25.00.

Plate 506. Demitasse Cup and Saucer, ceramic; red, blue, and green hand-painted dots on cream colored background, black trim; "Ivory Ware" by Hancock Pottery, England. $30.00 – 40.00.

Plate 507. Plate, 9"d, ceramic, facial profiles and crossed branches outlined in dark green on white body; Iroquois China Company, Syracuse, New York. $25.00 – 30.00

Plate 508. Dinner Plate, 10½" x 8"; Salad Plate, 6½" x 5¼"; Cup and Saucer, "Biarritz," marked "The Biarritz, Clarice Cliff, Royal Staffordshire Pottery, England." $250.00 – 275.00 set.

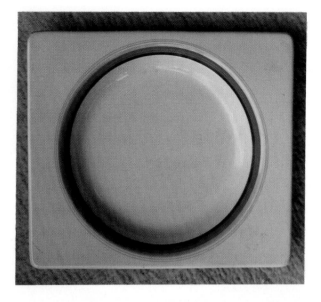

Plate 509. Soup Bowl, ceramic, rectangular shape; orange and black lines decorate inner border; marked "The Biarritz, Royal Stafford-shire Pottery, England." $45.00 – 55.00.

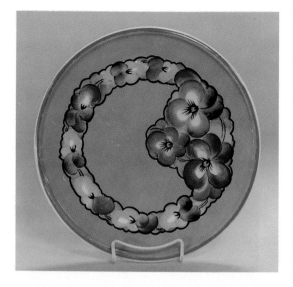

Plate 510. Tea Tile, 11½"d, ceramic, hand-painted pansy ring in vivid colors of red, blue, purple, and yellow outlined in black on turquoise background deco-rates center; narrow red border, Czechoslovakian. $75.00 – 85.00.

Plate 511. Cereal Bowls, 2"h x 5⅛"d, ceramic; "Ring" design in blue and rose, Bauer Pottery, Los Angeles, California. $18.00 – 20.00 each.

Plate 512. Covered Butter Dish, ceramic, green glaze, made by the Hall China Company, East Liverpool, Ohio. $45.00 – 55.00.

Plate 513. Gravy Boat, ceramic; "Fiesta Ware" in yellow, made by the Homer Laughlin Pottery, Newell, Virginia, ca. 1940s. $30.00 – 40.00.

Plate 514. Covered Serving Bowl, 8"d, ceramic; "Fiesta" in turquoise, Homer Laughlin Pottery. $150.00 – 200.00.

Plate 515. Pitcher, 7"h, ceramic, off-white glaze, made by the Red Wing Pottery, Red Wing, Minnesota, ca. 1930s. $50.00 – 65.00.

Plate 516. Water Pitcher, 7½"h, recessed band pattern on off-white body, made by the Alamo Pottery of San Antonio, Texas. $30.00 – 35.00.

Plate 517. Pitcher, 6½"h, ceramic "American Modern" design by Russel Wright for the Steubenville Pottery, Steubenville, Ohio, coral glaze, ca. 1940s. $100.00 – 125.00.

Plate 518. Covered Pitchers, 16"h and 6"h, matching Tray, 12"l, ceramic; green glaze with a molded leaf decor; Red Wing Pottery. $175.00 – 225.00 set.

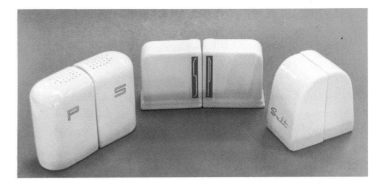

Plate 520. Salt and Pepper Shakers, ceramic, unmarked. $20.00 – 30.00 set.

Plate 519. This and the following picture show various Deco designs in Salt and Pepper Shakers ceramic, unmarked. $20.00 – 30.00 set.

Plate 521. Teapot, 7½"h, ceramic, yellow glaze with gold trim; "Moderne" pattern made by the Hall China Company, East Liverpool, Ohio. $50.00 – 65.00.

Plate 522. Teapot, 12½"h, ceramic, yellow glaze; "Ringware" pattern made by the Bauer Pottery of Los Angeles. $125.00 – 150.00.

Vases

Vases are designed for displaying floral arrangements, but as solitary objects they enhance a room's decor. Instead of being merely flower containers, they are considered art objects or decorative accessories, depending on their price. Like table wares, Deco vases were made of glass, metal, porcelain, or pottery. The photographs in this section are arranged in that order.

French art glass vases are the most expensive. Examples shown here include pieces by Daum, Legras, and Schneider. Other French manufacturers such as Baccarat, Lalique, and Gallé perhaps are more famous. But as their creations have become scarce and very costly, other factories' products have gained recognition. Consequently, most French art glass has moved entirely out of the range of the moderate collector.

For Deco image, however, less expensive vases made by European and American factories are quite pleasing. Much of this glass is unmarked and not attributable to any one factory. Lack of identification may serve the collector well when Deco shape rather than company or artist is the major concern. Czechoslovakian glass made between 1918 and 1939 has been gaining interest among Deco collectors for several years. Most of the pieces are marked "Czechoslovakia" or "Made in Czechoslovakia." The shapes and vivid colors of this good quality glass are quite representative of the Deco era. Prices usually remain moderate. Black milk glass or black amethyst glass made during the 1920s and 1930s is another type of relatively inexpensive glass with Deco overtones. Black glass was made by several American factories, but most pieces are unmarked.

American glassmakers such as Cambridge, Fostoria, Heisey, and New Martinsville, to name a few, are noted for stemware and serving dishes, but vases and other decorative items also were produced by these factories. Clear and colored glass vases were sometimes made to match the modern table ware patterns. Fan shapes, blocked geometric forms, and even etched nude designs project a Deco theme. Although this type of glass is avidly collected by Depression glass collectors, prices are far less than those for French art glass.

Metal adapts well to angular shapes. Although glass and ceramic vases are more common, those made of brass, bronze, copper, or chrome often evoke the Deco image in a more eye-catching way. The chrome vases pictured here are priced at the low end of the scale, but the Deco features are quite obvious. Brass and copper vases vary in price depending on size, but most are over $100. The sterling on bronze vases were made by the Heintz Art Metal Company. Increased interest over the last several years has caused prices to rise for this company's production. Examples are rarely less than $200 today. French bronze vases may be out of an affordable price range for moderate collectors. But an urn like the one shown, or similar vases, is usually considerably less than a bronze statue would cost. If French bronze would lend a note of prestige to one's collection, such vases are a good choice.

The most expensive ceramic vases are those made by European art potteries. Art pottery, however, usually is priced lower than art glass. This is apparent when prices are compared for the Amphora and Boch Frères ceramic vases with those for the Legras and Verlys glass examples. American art pottery is generally lower in price than European. Among American Art potteries, attention is being paid to the Deco production made by companies such as Roseville and Weller and others who implemented angular and streamlined designs during the 1920s and 1930s. A large selection of such pieces is included here. Less expensive vases are Japanese or American pottery varieties which were sold by dime stores or florists' shops. The angular white glazed Japanese vase shown here was originally cheap, but the striking Deco shape has caused its current value to increase sharply.

Porcelain vases are medium priced with few being either bargains or exorbitantly high. Porcelain is superior to simple pottery because it is stronger and translucent, but those qualities are not always reflected in prices. Most European porcelain vases are less expensive than European art pottery. The reason is because many decorative items such as urns, vases, and jardinieres were produced in quantity by porcelain factories. Moreover, they were often decorated with transfer designs or exported as undecorated vases. The latter were purchased by aspiring amateur china painters, and thus the decoration is not as creative or professional as that of art potteries.

Plate 524. Vase, 8½"h, smoke colored glass molded with designs commemorating the Maginot Line from World War I; Schneider Glass Factory, Epinay-sur-Seine, France. $1,200.00 – 1,400.00.

Plate 523. Vase, 16"h, glass, modernistic design in brown and amber; Legras factory, St. Denis, France, prior to 1914 (factory closing date), artist signed. $1,500.00 – 2,000.00.

Plate 525. Vase, 11"h, glass, flared neck with fancy scrolled handles; molded leaf decor highlighted with a hand-painted blue-green interior, Czechoslovakian, ca. 1920s. $350.00 – 400.00.

Plate 526. Vase, 7"h, black glass, triangular shaped neck; nude figures decorate base; L. E. Smith Glass Company, Mt. Pleasant, Pennsylvania, ca. 1930s. $80.00 – 100.00.

Plate 527. Vase, 12"h, black glass, trumpet shaped, unmarked, ca. 1930s. $55.00 – 65.00.

Plate 528. Vase, 7½"h, black glass, wide mouth with slightly tapered body; molded design on front imparts a three-dimensional effect, unmarked, American, ca. 1930s. $95.00 – 110.00.

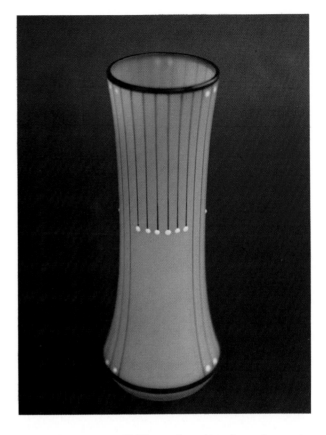

Plate 529. Vase, 6"h, black amethyst glass, hand painted, silver geometric decor, unmarked, American, ca. 1930s. $30.00 – 35.00.

Plate 530. Vase, 7½"h, pink satin glass decorated with black and white enameled work, marked "Made in Czechoslovakia," ca. 1930s. $60.00 – 75.00.

Plate 531. Vase, 8¼"h, clear glass designed with a flared upper body and stepped rings on lower section forming base; pink glass balls in graduated sizes decorate each side; Czechoslovakian, ca. 1930s. $125.00 – 150.00.

Plate 532. Vase, 6½"h, clear glass, "Cornucopia" pattern; New Martinsville Glass Company, New Martinsville, West Virginia. $40.00 – 50.00.

Plate 533. Vase, 8½"h, red glass in a "Rocket" design, New Martinsville Glass, ca. 1930s. $75.00 – 100.00.

Plate 534. Vase, 9"h, dark green glass, Zepplin-shaped base, unmarked, American. $65.00 – 75.00.

Plate 535. Vase, 9"h, light green glass with silver trim on legs and neck, unmarked. $90.00 – 100.00.

Plate 536. Vase, 10½"h, cobalt blue crystal shading from light to dark decorated with a girl juggling balls, painted in gold, unmarked, American. $65.00 – 75.00.

Plate 537. Vase, 10"h, rare crystal version of the "Tea Room" pattern by the Indiana Glass Company. $275.00 – 300.00.

Plate 538. Vase, 11½"h, vaseline glass in metal holder decorated with a dancing nude figure; Frankart Inc., New York City, ca. 1920s. $1,200.00 – 1,400.00.

Plate 539. Vase, 12"h, blown blue-green glass encased in wrought iron; Daum Glass Factory, Nancy, France. $1,500.00 – 2,000.00.

Plate 540. Vase, 17"h, bronzed metal and glass; three kneeling semi-nude figures surround metal part of vase which holds a flared pink glass insert, unmarked, American. $450.00 – 550.00.

Plate 541. Vase, 10½"h, brass with silver overlay in an abstract geometric pattern, artist signed "George," French. $600.00 – 700.00.

Plate 542. Planter, 4½"h, brass with applied cameo of a woman wearing an Egyptian style headdress, European, ca. 1920s. $70.00 – 90.00.

Plate 543. Vase, 4½"h x 7"w, bronze with acid wash patina forming abstract design, unmarked. $85.00 – 100.00.

Plate 544. Small Flower Bowl or Planter, 2"h, 5½"d; sterling floral design on bronze; Heintz Art Metal Co., Buffalo, New York, 1912 patent date with mark. (The following three examples are similarly marked.) $145.00 – 165.00.

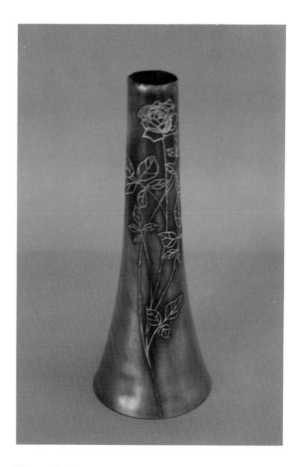

Plate 545. Vase, 12"h, slender stick style body with wide base, bronze, decorated with a sterling leaf design, Heintz. $275.00 – 325.00.

Plate 546. Vase, 12"h, sterling on bronze, geometric shaped roses and leaves decorate front, Heintz. $325.00 – 375.00.

Plate 547. Vase, 13"h, sterling on bronze, stylized chrysanthemums decorate front of upper body, Heintz. $350.00 – 400.00.

Plate 548. Urn, 8½"h, bronze, transitional elements of Art Nouveau and Art Deco, French. $400.00 – 500.00.

Plate 549. Pair of Vases, 8"h, hammered chrome, marked "Made in England." $140.00 – 160.00 pair.

Plate 551. Pair of Vases, 9"h, chrome, ribbed body design, unmarked. $45.00 – 55.00 pair.

Plate 550. Vase, 8¼"h, chrome, hammered body, unmarked. $65.00 – 75.00.

Plate 553. Pair of Vases, 13"h, copper, Egyptian influence, ca. late 1920s. $325.00 – 375.00 pair.

Plate 552. Wall Pocket Vase, 8"h, chrome, unmarked. $40.00 – 50.00.

Plate 554. Vase, porcelain, flared neck with a two-tiered scalloped molded design between base and mid section; hand decorated in yellow and shades of orange on white with gold trim; R. S. Tillowitz, ca. 1930s.

Plate 555. Vase, porcelain, red and white decor; handles shaped in a sharp stepped design; Reinhold Schlegelmilch Company, Tillowitz, Silesia (R. S. Tillowitz), ca. 1930s. $50.00 – 60.00.

Plate 556. Vase, 8½"h, porcelain, hand-painted Egyptian motif, Brauer Art Studio, Chicago. $200.00 – 250.00.

Plate 557. Vase, porcelain, red glaze on top and base with mid section decorated with a red diamond pattern on white body; R. S. Tillowitz, ca. 1930s. $80.00 – 90.00.

Plate 558. Wall Pocket Vase, pottery, made in the shape of a woman's head wearing a large hat, white glaze, unmarked. $80.00 – 100.00.

Plate 559. Vase, 7"h, pottery, stepped angular shape, white glaze, marked "Made in Japan." $30.00 – 35.00.

Plate 560. Vase, 7"h, pottery, abstract white, orange, and green floral design on yellow ground decorates top part of vase with a wide yellow band around the neck; artist signed "Lison," Boch Frères, Belgium. $300.00 – 350.00.

Plate 561. Vase, 14½"h, pottery, multicolored stylized floral decor around top and base of vase accented with cobalt blue trim, artist signed, marked "Amphora, Austria." $700.00 – 800.00.

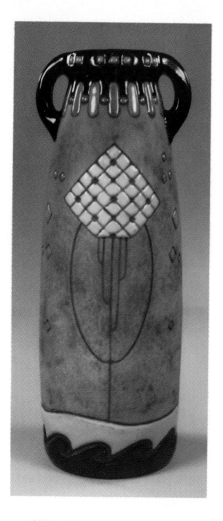

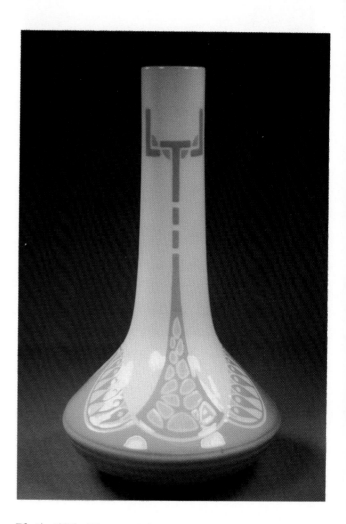

Plate 562. Vase, 13½"h, pottery, enameled geometric designs, cobalt blue trim, artist signed, marked "Amphora, Made in Czechoslovakia." $900.00 – 1,000.00.

Plate 563. Vase, 12"h, pottery, green and yellow abstract design on white body; Villeroy and Boch, Mettlach, Germany. $350.00 – 400.00.

Plate 564. Vase, 8"h, pottery, light brown zigzagged lines form a flame design around center of body with top of vase finished in red-orange shading to yellow; base and bottom part of vase finished in a dark blue; Ditmar Urbach Pottery, Czechoslovakia. $275.00 – 300.00.

Plate 565. Vase, 12"h, pottery, similar flame design as that on preceding vase except lower half of vase has a red-orange finish; Ditmar Urbach Pottery. $325.00 – 375.00.

Plate 566. Vase, 9"h, pottery, white glaze, abstract overlapping design decorates body; Abingdon Pottery, Abingdon, Illinois. $35.00 – 45.00.

Plate 567. Vase, 5"h x 8"w, pottery, wide modified fan shape, blue matt finish; Bauer Pottery, Los Angeles. $70.00 – 90.00.

Plate 568. Vase or Planter, 6½"h, 8"w, "Art Vellum" line in a mottled brown and green glaze, made by the Brush McCoy Pottery, Roseville, Ohio, ca. 1925. $125.00 – 145.00.

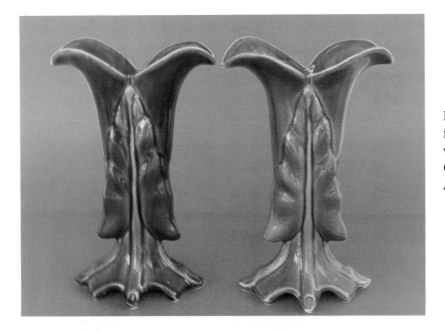

Plate 569. Pair of Vases, 11"h, pottery, stylized lily shape, dark green glaze, marked with "Camark" original paper label of the Camden Art and Tile Pottery, Camden, Arkansas. $75.00 – 100.00 pair.

Plate 570. Vase, 6½"h, 5½"w, pottery, stylized wild duck molded in relief on front with a cactus plant incised on reverse (not shown), honey tan glaze; Frankoma Pottery, Salpulpa, Oklahoma, ca. 1930s. $50.00 – 60.00.

Plate 571. Vase, 5¼"h x 6"w, "Early Art," line, turquoise glaze, made by Hull Pottery, Zanesville, Ohio, ca. 1920s – 1930s. $75.00 – 85.00.

Plate 572. Vase, Hull "Magnolia" pattern in pink and blue, matt finish, ca. 1940s. $200.00 – 250.00.

Plate 573. Vase, 6½"h, ceramic, mottled blue glaze, overlapping abstract design on front; made by Knowles, Taylor & Knowles, Burbank, California (KT&K Calif.), ca. late 1930s – 1940s. $35.00 – 45.00.

Plate 574. Vase, 7½"h, cornucopia shape juxta-posed to a wide base decorated with overlapping abstract designs in relief similar to that in preceding picture, blue glaze; KT&K Calif. $80.00 – 90.00.

Plate 575. Vase or Planter, 5½"h x 5½"w, incised leaf design, turquoise and raspberry finish; KT&K Calif. $45.00 – 55.00.

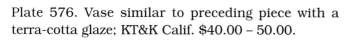

Plate 576. Vase similar to preceding piece with a terra-cotta glaze; KT&K Calif. $40.00 – 50.00.

Plate 577. Wall Pocket Vase, stylized floral design in relief, matt blue glaze; KT&K Calif. $40.00 – 50.00.

Plate 578. Vase; 5"h, 6"w, wide flared neck; white matt glaze on the exterior with interior decorated with a blue glaze; Rookwood Pottery, Cincinnati, Ohio. $225.00 – 250.00.

Plate 579. Vase, 4"h x 5"w, two handled, geometric shapes form border under neck, blue glaze; Rookwood Pottery. $265.00 – 285.00.

Plate 580. Vase, 5¼"h, simple abstract design on front, mauve color, matt finish; Rookwood. $225.00 – 250.00.

Plate 581. Vase, 5½"h, stylized peacock feather design, mauve, matt finish; Rookwood. $225.00 – 250.00.

Plate 582. Vase, 5¾"h, "Baneda" line, glossy pink and rose glaze; Roseville Pottery, Roseville, Ohio, ca. 1933. $375.00 – 425.00.

Plate 583. Jardiniere, 7"h x 6½"w, rare "Cameo" pattern, by Roseville; carved figures holding hands form decor around top half of piece. $575.00 – 625.00.

Plate 584. Vase, 3½"h x 4"w, "Cosmos" pattern by Roseville, ca. 1940s, two handled, green floral and leaf design on blue background. $150.00 – 175.00.

Plate 585. Double Bud Vase, 5"h x 8½"w, "Florentine" pattern in brown, Roseville, ca. mid to late 1920s. $175.00 – 200.00.

Plate 587. Jardiniere, 8½"h x 11½"w, "Futura," pink floral designs on gray body, Roseville. $1,000.00 – 1,200.00.

Plate 586. Footed Planter, 5½"h x 6¾"w, "Futura" line introduced by Roseville in 1928, stylized leaf design on pink and blue-green body. $700.00 – 800.00.

Plate 589. Hanging Basket, 8½"d, "Futura," rose colored leaves on gray background, Roseville. $650.00 – 750.00.

Plate 588. Vase, 5"h, "Futura," mottled rose-beige finish on body, decorated with a blue floral design, Roseville. $275.00 – 300.00.

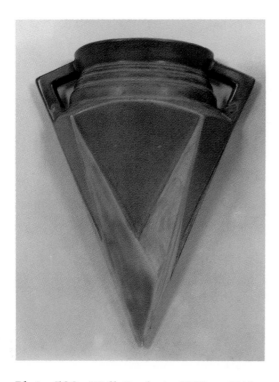

Plate 591. Window Box, 8½"l x 3½"w, "Gardenia" pattern, ca. 1940s, Roseville. $140.00 – 160.00.

Plate 590. Wall Pocket, 8½"l x 6½"w, triangular shape, "Futura," green, brown, and yellow finish, Roseville. $450.00 – 550.00.

Plate 592. Vase, 7"h, "Ivory" pattern by Roseville, ca. 1937. $70.00 – 80.00.

Plate 593. Vase, 5"h x 6½"w, "Ixia" pattern, white flowers on light pink background, Roseville, ca. 1930s. $200.00 – 225.00.

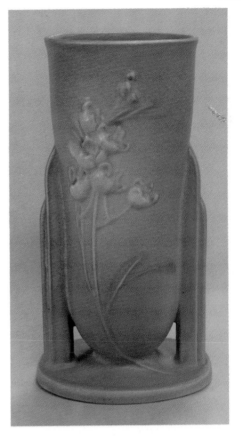

Plate 594. Vase, 8½"h, "Ixia" pattern on pink and blue background, stepped handles, Roseville, $250.00 – 275.00.

Plate 595. Vase, 7¼"h, "Ixia" pattern on yellow shading to pink body, Roseville. $200.00 – 225.00.

Plate 596. Vase, 7½"h, "Orian" line, ca. 1935; glossy rose glaze with blue-green interior, Roseville. $150.00 – 175.00.

Plate 597. Vase, 8¾"h, "Pinecone" design, ca. 1931, brown finish, Roseville. $225.00 – 250.00.

Plate 598. Vase, 6"h, cornucopia shape, "Pinecone" pattern, blue-green finish, Roseville. $200.00 – 225.00.

Plate 599. Vase, 6½"h, "Primrose" design, ca. 1932; white flowers on green body, Roseville. $150.00 – 175.00.

Plate 600. Vase, 6½"h x 6¾"w, "Snowberry" pattern, ca. 1946; small white flowers on green body, Roseville. $125.00 – 150.00.

Plate 601. Ewer, 10¾"h, "Snowberry" pattern, Roseville. $250.00 – 275.00.

Plate 603. Vase, 3¾"h x 6"w, turquoise blue, matt finish, unmarked, Roseville, ca. late 1920s. $60.00 – 75.00.

Plate 602. Vase, 9½"h, "Velmoss" line, green body glaze, Roseville, ca. 1935. $275.00 – 325.00.

Plate 604. Vase, 6¼"h, designed by George Rumrill and produced by Red Wing Pottery, Red Wing, Minnesota, ca. mid to late 1930s. $45.00 – 55.00.

Plate 605. Assortment of small Vases with "Turquoise-Blue" soft matt glaze made by the Van Briggle Pottery, Colorado Springs, Colorado, ca. 1920s – 1930s: left, 3"h x 3½"w, $75.00 – 100.00; middle, 5"h x 4½"w, $100.00 – 125.00; right, top hat, 2⅛"h x 3"w, $65.00 – 75.00.

Plate 606. Van Briggle Vase, 7¾"h, "Turquoise-Blue" glaze. $125.00 – 145.00.

Plate 607. Van Briggle Bud Vase, 9"h, "Turquoise-Blue" glaze. $50.00 – 65.00.

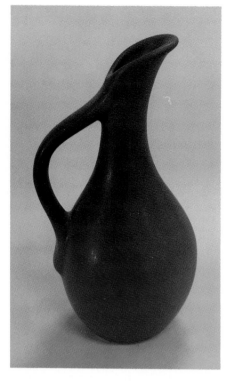

Plate 608. Van Briggle Ewer, 7"h, "Persian Rose" glaze. $150.00 – 175.00.

Plate 609. Van Briggle Pitcher, 5¼"h, heart-shaped mouth, "Persian Rose" glaze. $300.00 – 350.00.

Plate 610. Vase, 8½"h, "Cameo" pattern, large white flowers in relief on tan body; Weller Pottery, Zanesville, Ohio, ca. late 1930s. $65.00 – 75.00.

Plate 612. Planter, 7½" x 8", round body with open work design on top half, "Klyro" pattern, small pink and green floral design on ivory body, Weller. $100.00 – 125.00.

Plate 611. Figural Planter, 7½"h, nude figure with drape, "Hobart" line, Weller Pottery, Zanesville, Ohio. $175.00 – 200.00.

Plate 613. Pitcher, 8½"h, "Oak Leaf" design by Weller, ca. 1930s, green leaves on shaded brown background. $100.00 – 120.00.

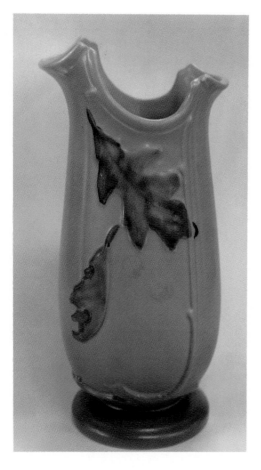

Plate 615. Weller "Oak Leaf" double Bud Vase, 6½"h x 7"w. $100.00 – 120.00.

Plate 614. Weller "Oak Leaf" Vase, 11"h. $120.00 – 140.00.

Plate 616. Vase, 8"h, "Roba" line by Weller; white flower with green leaves in relief on green body, ca. late 1930s. $80.00 – 95.00.

Reproductions

Reproductions can be found in practically all collecting fields. Art Deco reproductions have not just recently appeared. Bronze figures are probably the most reproduced Art Deco items. Many of these have been on the market for more than a decade. Today, one only has to look through trade newspapers and magazines to see advertisements for various companies offering such items. Pictures are usually included with the ad, and one can send for catalogs of the various wholesalers or manufacturers. Most of the new figures are based on the original works of famous European designers of the era. Although advertised as manufactured with the "lost wax" method and sporting the same or similarly spelled names of such artists as Chiparus, Zach, or Preiss, these bronzes are still only replicas and not from the period. Unfortunately, they are sometimes sold as authentic sculptures by antique dealers or by some auction companies.

While taking photographs for the first edition of this book some years ago, I encountered some misrepresentations. One example was a "Footsteps" figure with a signature of "D. H. Chaparus." The price was about $1,700.00. An original would have been many times that figure. But that amount was still a hefty mark up from the wholesale price of about $250.00. (The figure in question was not the one shown in this section by the same title.) Also, a knowledgeable collector would have been quick to note that "Chiparus" was misspelled. Today, prices for such reproductions are usually more in line with the expected difference between wholesale and retail, and thus, it is evident to most collectors that the statues are new.

Be aware of the very high prices of originals and also the limited availability of originals. While such pieces may come on the market through auctions or private dealers, they are not likely to turn up at most antique shops. A selection of a number of sculptures of different designs at one shop, all priced similarly, is usually another clue that the pieces are reproductions. Modern reproductions are okay if one wishes to purchase such an item for enjoyment at a fraction of the price of the original and knows that the piece is a reproduction. Too often, though, collectors can get "burned" if they are new to a particular collecting field, or if they are too eager to find a bargain. I receive many letters from individuals who purchased porcelain reproductions such as Limoges or R. S. Prussia. In many cases, I think they suspect the china is not authentic and thus write for verification. Those bargains often turn out to be costly mistakes.

A few examples of reproduced figures are shown here. These pieces were for sale at a retail outlet. Each piece was tagged with the price and name of an original designer. The prices were clearly indicative that the figures were not originals. The dealer was not trying to fool his customers. I have listed the general price rather than the exact figure which was on the tag along with the artist or company name in parentheses. You will note that the prices are around $200.00 to $300.00 for each figure, and those prices will vary from outlet to outlet. Because of the proliferation of these sculptures, mispresentation is not as common today. Trade with reputable dealers who will refund your money if you are not satisfied with the purchase.

Plate R1. "The Butterfly Dancer," 16"h (Chiparus), $250.00.

Plate R2. "Girl with Parrot,"
15¼"h (P. Phillippe), $290.00.

Plate R3. "La Cavache," 13"h
(The Riding Crop, Bruno
Zach), $290.00.

Plate R4. "Kapthuria," 12½"h (Chiparus),
$290.00.

Plate R5. "Peirrot with Lute,"
14"h (Chiparus), $350.00.

Plate R6. "Footsteps,"
16½"h (Chiparus),
$280.00.

Plate R7. "Nymph Lamp," 15"h with shade 8¾"d
(Frankart), $180.00.

Index to Manufacturers and Marks

Bibliography

Arwas, Victor. *Art Deco*. New York: Harry N. Abrams, Inc., 1980.

Baker, Lillian. *Art Nouveau & Art Deco Jewelry*. Paducah, Kentucky: Collector Books, 1981.

Blasberg, Robert W. and Carol L. Bohdan. *Fulper Art Pottery*. New York: The Jordan-Volpe Gallery, n.d.

Battersby, Martin. *The Decorative Twenties*. New York: Walker and Company. 1969.

Brunhammer, Yvonne. *The Nineteen Twenties Style*. London: Paul Hamlyn, 1969.

Cummings, Urban K. *Ronson*. Palo Alto, CA: Bird Dog Books, 1992.

Duncan, Alastair. *Art Deco Furniture and the French Designers*. New York: Holt, Rinehart and Winston. 1984.

Florence, Gene. *The Collector's Encyclopedia of Depression Glass*. Paducah, Kentucky: Collector Books, 1979.

_____. *Elegant Glassware of the Depression Era*. Paducah, Kentucky: Collector Books, 1983.

Forsythe, Ruth A. *Made in Czechoslovakia*. Galena, Ohio: Ruth A. Forsythe, 1982.

Fredgant, Don. *Collecting Art Nouveau: Identification and Value Guide*. Florence, Alabama: Books Americana, 1982.

Fusco, Tony. *Official Identification and Price Guide Art Deco*, First Edition. New York: House of Collectibles, 1989.

Gaston, Mary Frank. *Antique Brass*. Paducah, Kentucky: Collector Books, 1985.

_____. *Antique Copper*. Paducah, Kentucky: Collector Books, 1985.

_____. *Haviland Collectibles and Objects of Art*. Paducah, Kentucky: Collector Books, 1984.

Gerson, Roselyn. *Ladies' Compacts*. Radnor, PA: Wallace-Homestead Book Company, 1989.

Godden, Geoffrey. *Encyclopedia of British Pottery and Porcelain Marks*. New York: Crown Publishers, 1964.

Greif, Martin. *Depression Modern: The Thirties Style in America*. New York: Universe Books, 1975.

Haslam, Malcolm. *Collectors Style Guide Art Deco*. New York: Ballantine Books, 1987.

Hillier, Bevis. *Art Deco of the 20's and 30's* [rev. ed.]. New York: Schocken Books, 1985.

_____. *Minneapolis Institute of the Arts Catalog: The World of Art Deco*. New York: E.P. Dutton, 1971.

_____. *The Decorative Arts of the Forties and Fifties*. New York: Clarkson N. Potter, Inc., 1975.

Hull, John. *Art Deco*. San Francisco: Troubador Press, 1975.

Husfloen, Kyle (ed.). *1995 Antique & Collectibles Price Guide*. Dubuque, IA: Antique Trader Books, 1995.

_____. *1996 Antique & Collectibles Price Guide*. Dubuque, IA: Antique Trader Books, 1996.

Huxford, Sharon and Bob [eds.]. *Schroeder's Antiques Price Guide*. Paducah, Kentucky: Collector Books, 1988.

_____. *Schroeder's Antique Price Guide*. Paducah, KY: Collector Books, 1996.

Jervis, Simon. *The Facts on File: Dictionary of Design and Designers*. New York: Facts on File, Inc., 1984.

Kilbride, Richard S. *Art Deco Chrome the Chase Era*. Stamford, CT: Jo-D Books, 1988.

_____. *Art Deco Chrome Book 2*. Stamford, CT: Jo-D Books, 1992.

Klein, Dan. *Art Deco*. London: Treasure Press, 1984.

Kovel, Ralph and Terry. *The Kovel's Antiques & Collectibles Price List*. New York: Crown Publishers, Inc., 1987.

Lehner, Lois. *Ohio Pottery and Glass Marks and Manufacturers*. Des Moines, Iowa: Wallace-Homestead Book Co., 1978.

Lesieutre, Alain. *The Spirit and Splendor of Art Deco*. New York: Paddington Press Ltd., 1974.

McClinton, Katherine Morrison. *Art Deco: A Guide for Collectors*. New York: Clarkson N. Potter, Inc., 1972; rev. ed. 1986.

McConnell, Kevin. "The Heintz Art Metal Shop's Great Bronze Age." *The Antique Trader Price Guide to Antiques*, 1990.

Maenz, Paula. *Art Deco 1920–1940.* Koln: Veriag M. DuMont, 1974.

Marion, Frieda and Norma Werner. *Dresser Dolls and Other China Figurals.* Paducah, KY: Collector Books, 1983.

Menten, Theodore. *The Art Deco Style.* New York: Dover Publications, Inc., 1972.

_____. *Advertising Art in the Art Deco Style.* New York: Dover Publications, Inc., 1975.

Miller, Martin and Judith. *Miller's Antiques Price Guide.* Cranbrook, England: M.J.M. Publications, Ltd., 1985.

Murphy, Catherine and Kyle Husfloen [eds.]. *The Antique Trader Antiques and Collectibles Price Guide.* Dubuque, Iowa: Babka Publishing Co., 1987.

Röntgen, Robert E. *Marks on German, Bohemian and Austrian Porcelain: 1710 to present.* Exton, Pennsylvania: Schiffer Publishing Co., 1981.

Scarlett, Frank and Marjorie Townley. *Arts Decoratifs 1925.* London: St. Martin's Press, 1975.

Sembach, Klaus Jorgen. *Style 1930.* New York: Universe Books, 1971.

Sferrazza, Julie. *Farber Brothers Krome Kraft.* Marietta, OH: Antique Publications, 1988.

Sloan, Jean. *Perfume & Scent Bottle Collecting,* Second Edition. Radnor, PA: Wallace-Homestead Book Company, 1989.

Van Hook, Barry L. *Art Deco Reflections.* Vol. 1–Vol 3. #6, April 1991–February/March, 1994.

Veronesi, Giulia. *Style and Design 1909–1929.* New York: George Braziller, 1968.

Warman's 1987 Antiques and Their Prices. Willow Grove, Pennsylvania: Warman Publishing Co., Inc., 1987.

Watson, Howard and Pat. *The Colorful World of Clarice Cliff.* London: Kevin Francis Publishing, 1992.

_____. *Collecting Art Deco Ceramics.* London: Kevin Francis Publishing, 1993.

Weinstein, Iris and Robert K. Brown. *Art Deco Internationale.* New York: Quick Fox, 1977.

Woodard, Dannie A. and Billie J. Wood. *Hammered Aluminum Hand Wrought Collectibles.* Wolfe City, Texas: Henington Publishing Co., 1983.